Words and Structure

CSLI Lecture Notes
Number 151

Words and Structure

Jane Grimshaw

CSLI
PUBLICATIONS

Center for the Study of
Language and Information
Stanford, California

Copyright © 2005
CSLI Publications
Center for the Study of Language and Information
Leland Stanford Junior University
Printed in the United States
09 08 07 06 05   1 2 3 4 5

Library of Congress Cataloging-in-Publication Data

Grimshaw, Jane B. (Jane Barbara), 1951–
Words and structure / by Jane Grimshaw.

p. cm. – (CSLI lecture notes ; no. 151)

Includes bibliographical references and index.
ISBN 1-57586-422-3 (pbk. : alk. paper)
ISBN 1-57586-421-5 (hard. : alk. paper)

1. Lexicology. 2. Semantics. 3. Language acquisition. I. Title. II. Series.

P326.G68 2003
413′.028–dc21   2003013984
CIP

CSLI was founded in 1983 by researchers from Stanford University, SRI
International, and Xerox PARC to further the research and development of
integrated theories of language, information, and computation. CSLI headquarters
and CSLI Publications are located on the campus of Stanford University.

CSLI Publications reports new developments in the study of language,
information, and computation. Please visit our web site at
http://cslipublications.stanford.edu/
for comments on this and other titles, as well as for changes
and corrections by the author and publisher.

To A.P., A.P. and John Golfinos

Contents

Acknowledgements

"Extended Projection" is a revision of a paper originally written in 1991, and informally circulated. Part of the material in Sections 1.1–1.4 appeared in a slightly different form as Grimshaw 2000. This research was supported by the National Science Foundation under award #8808286 ("Conceptual Structure and Argument Structure in a Natural Language Lexicon") to Brandeis University, Ray Jackendoff and Jane Grimshaw Principal Investigators, and award #8819857 ("Lexical Representation of Non-Local Selectional Dependencies") to New York University, Mark Baltin Principal Investigator. Thanks to David Adger, Mark Baltin, Claudia Borgonovo, Daniel Büring, José Camacho, Peter Cole, Stanley Dubinsky, Tom Ernst, Bob Frank, Katerina Hartmann, Gabriella Hermon, Arild Hestvik, Henrietta Hung, Soowon Kim, Chungmin Lee, Jim McCloskey, Heizo Nakajima, Ad Neeleman, Ray Jackendoff, Christer Platzack, Alan Prince, Geoff Pullum, Marga Reis, Johan Rooryck, Sara Rosen, Vieri Samek-Lodovici, Roger Schwarzschild, Magui Suñer, Hubert Truckenbrodt, Saeko Urushibara, Sten Vikner, Edwin Williams and Cheryl Zoll. Versions of this work were presented between 1989 and 1991 at the University of Southern California, the University of Connecticut, MIT, the University of Texas at Austin, the University of Toronto, the University of Düsseldorf, the University of Leiden, the University of Stuttgart, Utrecht University, the West Coast Conference on Formal Linguistics, and in courses at the 1991 Linguistic Society of America Institute at the University of California at Santa Cruz, and at the Instituto Universitario Ortega y Gasset. Discussions in these numerous forums shaped the work in many important ways.

The ideas developed in "Semantic Structure and Semantic Content in Lexical Representation" build on a line of research initiated in Pinker 1989, and pursued by both Pinker and myself in several talks and papers, including Grimshaw and Pinker 1989, Grimshaw 1994 and Pinker 1994. Comments from Lila Gleitman, Beth Levin, and from audiences at the University of Maryland and the University of Texas, have played an important part in the work. This paper was circulated informally in 1993.

I gratefully acknowledge permission to reprint the following chapter: "Form, Function and the Language Acquisition Device." It originally appeared in C. L. Baker and J. J. McCarthy eds. *The Logical Problem of Language Acquisition.* Copyright © 1981 by MIT Press. Reprinted by permission.

The material in "Datives, Feet and Lexicons" Section 4.1, "The Semantic Properties of the Alternation" summarizes the argument of Grimshaw 1989. It was first presented as "The Acquisition of Verbs and Argument Structure: Comments" at the Boston University Language Development Conference, October 1987. This research was supported by the National Science Foundation under grant IST-8420073 to Brandeis University.

The research reported in "Datives, Feet and Lexicons" Section 4.2 "The Prosodic Properties of the Verbs" was supported by grant IST-8420073 from the National Science Foundation to Brandeis University and by BRSG S07 RR0744 awarded by the Biomedical Research Support Grant Program, Division of Research Resources, National Institutes of Health. It was presented under the title "Remarks on Dative Verbs and Universal Grammar," at the Boston University Language Development Conference in 1985. The analysis was partly developed in collaboration with Alan Prince, and has sometimes been referred to as a co-authored work in progress, under the title "A prosodic account of the *to*-dative alternation."

An earlier version of "Datives, Feet and Lexicons" Section 4.3 "English Speakers as Lexical Bilinguals" was presented under the title "English Speakers as Lexical Bilinguals" at the Boston University Language Development Conference / Linguistic Society of America, January 1994, and at the XV Symposium on Spanish and Portuguese Bilingualism, Rutgers University, February 1995.

My sincere thanks go to Dikran Karagueuzian, Christine Sosa, Lauri Kanerva and Tony Gee at CSLI Publications for their assistance and, most emphatically, for their patience. Jessica Rett, in her role as manuscript maven, made it possible for the book to be finished.

Works Cited in Acknowledgements

See References on page 129 for publication information on the following works cited in Acknowledgements.

Baker and McCarthy eds. 1981
Grimshaw 1989, 1994, 2000
Grimshaw and Pinker 1989
Pinker 1989, 1994

1

Extended Projection

1.1 Introduction

One of the most fundamental developments in the theory of phrase structure has involved the extension of X-bar theory beyond the familiar lexical categories, such as N, V, and A. This extension is made possible by recognizing that elements belonging to the minor syntactic categories, like complementizer, determiner, and even some bound morphemes, like inflection, are X-zero level categories for X-bar theory and consequently head their own projections. This position is taken in Jackendoff 1977. The second step in the development involves dividing the syntactic categories into two groups, the "lexical" categories and the "functional" categories. Roughly, the lexical class includes the major syntactic categories, the functional class the minor categories. The third step in the reasoning hypothesizes that the lexical categories and their projections characteristically occur enclosed within functional projections, as complements to functional heads (Chomsky 1986a, Fassi Fehri 1987, Fukui 1986, Fukui and Speas 1986, Abney 1987). In this analysis the head of an expression composed of a functional head (an "F-head") and a lexical head (an "L-head") plus their projections, is functional, and not lexical.

This version of the theory of phrase structure allows the extension of the standard principles of X-bar theory to many elements such as determiners and complementizers which previously fell outside it, in the sense that the theory said nothing interesting about them. In the current theory, these F-heads are complement-taking items, just as L-heads are. Each zero level category now heads a maximal projection. Every phrase is the maximal projection of some zero level category. In the simplest case, every phrase has the same internal structure: head final at the XP level and head initial at the X-bar level in the case of English. Every head is in principle complement-taking.

The functional-head hypothesis has proved particularly fruitful in the domain of clause structure, where it solves the long-standing problem of how S′ and S fit with X-bar theory (Hornstein 1977; Fassi Fehri 1987; Chomsky 1986a). The other major research area has been the structure of the nominal system, where evidence has been growing to show that what was previously taken to be the projection of an N is really the projection of a D, i.e. a "DP" (Brame 1981, 1982; Hellan 1985; Fukui 1986; Abney 1987; Ritter 1987).

In a theory which posits heads and projections of two different kinds, what combinations are possible? Can any L-head take any functional projection as its complement? Can any F-head take any lexical projection as its complement? The more heads there are, the more logically possible combinations there are. The idea to be explored here is that a proper subset of the logically possible combinations have a special property: they form what I will call "extended projections."

1.2   Extended Projection

Extended Projection involves an extended notion of an X-bar theoretic *projection*, in which noun-headed constituents and verb-headed constituents form (extended) projections, which include both the projection of their lexical heads and the functional shell which surrounds the lexical projection. This idea can be made precise by exploiting a feature analysis of the kind familiar from work on X-bar theory. The key is the hypothesis that the same category features are assigned to N and the functional heads which occur above it, including D, and more controversially, P. Hence these heads are of the same syntactic category, once we abstract away from the lexical/functional distinction. (There are many complexities in the behavior of P which I address below in Section 1.4.6.) V, I and C also have identical category features, which are different of course from those of N and D. Similarly adverbs and adjectives each have their own distinct feature analysis, although I will largely ignore them here, except for Section 1.4.5.

The two crucial components of Extended Projection are the idea that projections of lexical heads form larger projections of some kind with the functional heads above them, and that the formation of such projections depends on identity of category. These core ideas are shared with the proposals in Abney 1987, Haider 1988 and van Riemsdijk 1990, 1998[1]. The two components are logically independent as far as I can tell: it is possible that a larger projection is formed above a lexically

---

[1]Nakajima (1991) posits the same categorial relationships based on properties of extraction.

headed phrase, but that this is not based on category. It is also possible that categorial identity holds between N, D and P, but that no larger projections are formed among them.

For the sake of concreteness, I will simply designate the feature complex of N, D and P as [nominal], and that of V, I and C as [verbal]. Several feature systems in the literature would be at least broadly compatible with the proposals here. Jackendoff (1977) posits a feature system in which, for example, N and Art have systematically related features. Both are [+Subj, −Obj], giving them in essence, category identity. N is [+Comp] and Art is [−Comp], encoding a lexical/functional distinction. Abney (1987) posits the features [−N] for V, I and C, and [+N] for N and D. For a variety of other hypotheses concerning features see Muysken 1983, Holmberg 1986, Reuland 1986 and Haeberli 2001. The choice of feature analysis is crucial: for example feature systems which group arguments (DP, CP and possibly others) together as opposed to predicates (V and others) are inconsistent with category identity of V and C[2]. Some details are not important, however, provided that identity of category among the relevant heads is preserved. In support of identity, van Riemsdijk (1990) points out that articles are often similar in form to nominal entities such as clitics, pronouns and demonstratives, and that words which realize inflectional material associated with verbs tend to be verb-like in their properties, auxiliary verbs being an example.

Since functional heads are of the same category as their lexical counterparts, what distinguishes them is their functional status, encoded as a value for the feature F. $F0$ is assigned to the lexical categories, $F1$ to the lowest level functional category (D, and I so far); and $F2$ to the next (so far C and P); and so forth. The functional value of a node is independent of its categorial analysis. There are several reasons for this. First, the value of F plays a role in the formation of extended projections which is different from that played by the categorial features. Second, F is not a binary feature. Third, F is cross-categorial: it does not interact with the categorial features in any way. These points will be illustrated shortly. In the meantime, we can simply note that the functional feature resembles the X-bar theoretic level value, which distinguishes X-zero from X-bar from X-double bar.

---

[2]Cases where category appears to be neutralized (see Lefebvre and Muysken 1988, Lefebvre and Massam 1988, Plann 1986 and Section 1.4.5) provide further constraints on the set of features. The noun/verb distinction seems to be readily neutralizable, supporting a feature system in which they have significant properties in common, rather than being conceived of as maximally opposing elements, as in the feature system of Chomsky 1970a.

The categorial theory which forms the basis for Extended Projection makes explicit the hypothesis that a functional category is a *relational* entity. It is a functional category by virtue of its relationship to a lexical category. DP, for example, is a functional category *for N*, as IP is *for V*. A category label is now a pair consisting of a categorial specification, and a functional specification.

(1) a.   V   [+V −N] $F0$
     b.   I   [+V −N] $F1$
     c.   C   [+V −N] $F2$

(2) a.   N   [−V +N] $F0$
     b.   D   [−V +N] $F1$
     c.   P   [−V +N] $F2$

We can define a *head* and a *projection* as in (3) and (4):

(3)   X is a *head* of YP, and YP is a *projection* of X iff:

a. YP dominates X

b. The categorial features of YP and X are consistent

c. There is no inconsistency in the categorial features of all nodes intervening between X and YP (where a node N *intervenes* between X and YP if YP dominates X and N, N dominates X.)

In addition to the matching of categories of the elements in a projection, they must also have a particular relationship in terms of F-value. Two possible ways of stating this are given in (4). They are empirically distinct (see Sections 1.3 and 1.4.6). However, either one will entail the basic result we seek.[3]

(4)   Either:
      The F-value of X is lower than the F-value of YP
      or:
      The F-value of X is not higher than the F-value of YP[4]

I will refer to the second option in (4) as the "no increase" version. The

---

[3]In Grimshaw 1991, the original version of this paper, the F-value of the complement to a functional head was required to be lower than the F-value of the head itself.

[4]The definition in Grimshaw 2000 offers the following instead of (4): "No node intervening between X and YP is lexical." However, I believe that the present version is preferable: it derives the fact that lexical heads do not form extended projections with their complements from the same condition that requires higher-valued heads to occur higher in an extended projection than lower-valued. In addition, the 2000 version of the definition will allow YP to be lexical, assuming that it does not count as intervening between X and itself. This is not the right result.

two formulations differ in whether or not a head and a complement with the same F-value form an extended projection (see below and Section 1.4.6).

The standard notion of head and projection, which I will refer to as a "perfect head/projection," is obtained by imposing the additional requirement that F-values be shared within a projection.

(5)   X is a *perfect head* of YP, and YP is a *perfect projection* of X iff:
      X is a head of YP and the F-value of X is the same as the
      F-value of YP

Thus the familiar definition of a head and a projection requires identical category status and identical functional status. D is the head of DP because the two nodes have the same category and they match in functional level. N is not, however, the perfect head of DP, because the two nodes differ in functional level, or F-value in the present terms.

A noun and the functional projections which form a shell around it count as a single (extended) projection, as does a verb and its functional shell, because of their categorial uniformity. For example, DP is a perfect projection of D and D′, which it shares both categorial and functional features with, but not of N, N′, or NP, which it shares just category features with. It is, however, a (extended) projection of N, N′ and NP, as well as of D and D′. Crucially, the fact that the components of the (extended) projection are not uniform with respect to F-value does not prevent them from forming a projection, provided that identity of categorial features is preserved.

(6)

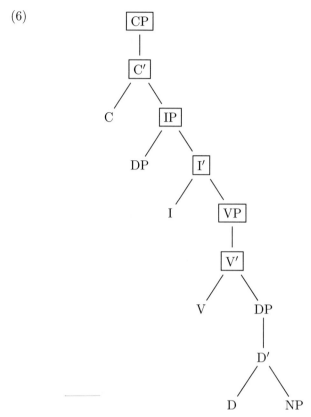

Under this proposal, then, a phrase can be simultaneously a configurational complement to a head, and part of the same (extended) projection.[5] The boxed nodes in (6) form a single verbal extended projection. The IP in (6) is a complement to C and also part of the CP projection; the VP is a complement to I and part of the same extended projection. Both V and I are (extended) heads of CP.

However, the definition of an extended projection is not satisfied where a head and its complement differ in syntactic category, and thus a VP containing a V and a direct object DP does not form a single extended projection. (Since adjectives and adverbs are categorially distinct from nouns and verbs, and from each other, they will each form their own extended projection, along with any degree elements. See Section 1.4.5.) Morever, although an IP and the VP complement to its head I do count as a single extended projection, a VP and an IP

---

[5]It may be necessary to add the requirement that only complements, and not specifiers of L-heads or F-heads, participate in extended projections.

EXTENDED PROJECTION / 7

complement to its head V does not. V can be the (extended) head of IP, since the F-value of I is higher than that of V, but I cannot be an (extended) head of VP, because the F-value of V is lower than that of I.

With the possible exception of lexical heads taking matching lexical projections as complements, discussed below, lexical heads never form extended projections with the functional or lexical projections which are their complements, since lexical heads have the lowest F-value. Apart from the just-mentioned exception, an L-head and its perfect projection are always the most deeply embedded members of any extended projection, and the complement of an L-head is always the top of a new extended projection. By the same reasoning, a phrase with the highest F-value (here CP and PP) will never form a projection with a phrase on top of it. (4) prevents the formation of an extended projection in instances where a lexical head takes a functional projection as complement, and where a functional head takes a functional category with a higher F-value.

This second essential component of Extended Projection, the hypothesis that a larger projection can be formed from a combination of lexical and functional projections, is common, as mentioned above, to several works: Haider 1988, van Riemsdijk 1990, 1998, Abney 1987 and Radford 1993.[6] There are, however, important differences among these various proposals.

Abney introduces the concept of a semantic projection: "A node's s-projection is the path of nodes along which its descriptive content is 'passed along.'" (Abney 1987: 39). Functional heads form s-projections with their complements. The s-projection is thus a semantic counterpart to an extended projection, as defined here. A syntactic projection, as defined by Abney, is equivalent to a perfect projection in this work. So there is a major difference between these two hypotheses; whether the relationship between a lexical head and the functional projections above it is syntactic, as well as semantic.

Haider (1988) argues that functional projections have a privileged relationship to projections they contain, forming a kind of virtual projection superimposed on the lower projection. As a result, an element in the specifier of e.g. an IP can act as if it is the specifier of a higher projection, such as a CP. While the problems considered by Haider are disjoint from those considered here, the idea seems to be fundamentally similar.

---

[6]The unification of information from the entire verbal projection in LFG proposals is closely related, relying on the idea that sisters of F-heads are "co-heads." See, e.g. Austin and Bresnan 1996: 221–222.

According to Radford (1993), nominal structures have multiple heads, all of which must agree with each other (see Section 1.4.2). Radford's "ultimate head" is an extended lexical head in the theory proposed here. The proposals differ as to what counts as a head of a nominal phrase: An adjectival modifier is a head of the nominal under Radford's hypothesis, for example, but forms a distinct extended projection headed by a degree head (see Section 1.4.5) in the present theory.

In a pair of papers, van Riemsdijk (1990, 1998) proposes and then clarifies a particular hypothesis concerning the nature of the projections formed by functional structure over lexical heads. In his view, what I treat as an extended projection is just a projection, but one with multiple heads. There are two central differences between van Riemsdijk's view and Extended Projection. First, I argue here that PP and CP are extended projections of N and V (although see Section 1.4.6 for discussion). van Riemsdijk's proposal is that DP and IP are projections, but the hypothesis does not encompass P and C. A second important difference concerns specifier positions: van Riemsdijk (1998) emphasizes that a projection admits only a single specifier, which occurs at the highest level, hence there can be no specifier position within a lexical projection, or any functional projection other than the top one. This seems inconsistent with a number of other ideas, such as the "VP shell" hypothesis (Larson 1988) which posits multiple specifier positions within VP, the availability of multiple specifier positions for object shift (Bobaljik and Jonas 1996), and the argument in Cinque 1999 that adverbs are generated in the specifier position of functional projections, an incompatibility noted by van Riemsdijk himself.

There are significant differences within this group of hypotheses, but still a fundamental shared core. The core concerns the nature of the problem of determining the proper head for a phrase. Why was it difficult, having recognized the concept of a head, to determine whether the D or the N was the head of a nominal constituent, for example? The answer is that in some sense both are heads of the nominal: it is a bigger version of both D and N. Thus a more refined theory, which distinguishes among types of heads, is called for.

1.3 Possible Head Complement Relations

In principle, any combination of heads and complements is allowed by X-bar theory, as noted in the introduction. Extended Projection makes it possible to restrict combinations in a principled way.

The head-complement combinations in (7), which involve lexical heads, are either attested or (like N with a DP complement) ruled out by independent principles of the theory. Fundamentally, L-heads take complements of all syntactic categories and F-values, modulo independent well-formedness conditions such as case theory. This was pointed out in Abney 1987.

(7) V-PP, V-DP, V-NP, V-CP, V-IP, V-VP[7]
     N-PP, N-DP, N-NP, N-CP, N-IP, N-VP

Certain head-complement relations where the head is functional are uncontroversially possible: those in (8), for example.

(8) C-IP, I-VP
     P-DP, D-NP

The categorial identity of C, I and V on the one hand, and P, D and N on the other, means that the combinations in (8) are all extended projections by the definition in (3) and (4). Other combinations of a functional head and a complement, those in (9), fail to meet the definition, by virtue of a categorial discrepancy or F-value, or both. In these cases, the theory posits two independent projections, rather than a single extended projection.[8]

(9) I-NP, I-DP, I-PP, I-CP
     D-VP, D-IP, D-CP, D-PP
     C-NP, C-DP
     P-VP, P-IP
     I-IP, D-DP

Many of them (such as I-CP, D-PP, I-PP, C-DP), are completely unattested and not independently excluded. The position I will take here is that the combinations in (9) are all impossible, despite the fact that a few of them have been posited for particular constructions with mixed properties, to be analyzed further in Section 1.4.5. Our conclusion has to be that unlike L-heads, each F-head occurs only with a very limited set of complements, quite typically only with one, as indeed Abney (1987) noted. This follows if *F-heads take only complements that they form extended projections with*, while L-heads are not required to form extended projections with their complements (indeed they cannot do so). If we break up I (or indeed any of the other functional heads) into a set of heads, the number of combinations increases, but the logic of the argument stays the same.

---

[7]Throughout the paper, the notation X-YP stands for X with a YP complement. The notation XP-YP stands for an XP containing a YP complement to X.

[8]If C-VP and P-NP are excluded, it must be for reasons independent of Extended Projection, since heads with non-adjacent F-values can form extended projections. See Sections 1.5 and 1.6, where the relevant cases are analyzed.

The ill-formed head-complement combinations in (9) are ruled out by a version of the theta criterion which recruits *Extended Projection*, intended to apply to adjuncts and matrix clauses as well as arguments.

(10)   Generalized Theta Criterion[9]
        Every maximal projection must be part of an extended
        projection that receives a role.

The criterion can be satisfied in two ways. A maximal projection at the top of an extended projection which receives a role satisfies the definition, since it is part of an extended projection which receives a role. (Note that this is true even if the maximal projection in question is the only element in the extended projection.) A maximal projection which is inside an extended projection which receives a role also satisfies the definition.

A lexical head assigns a role to the maximal projection which acts as its complement. This is why the combinations in (7) are legitimate. The combinations in (8) are potentially legitimate; the maximal projection is part of a larger extended projection. Provided that the entire extended projection is assigned a role, every maximal projection in that extended projection will meet the Generalized Theta Criterion. However, the combinations in (9) do not have the potential to meet the criterion. The maximal projections do not themselves receive a role, since they are complements to F-heads. Moreover, they do not form an extended projection with the structure above them, so they cannot be legitimized in this way. Thus a combination like a C with a DP complement, which cannot form an extended projection, is impossible. The DP is neither a complement to a lexical head, nor part of an extended projection which includes CP.

This is the explanation for Abney's observation that lexical heads, but not functional heads, take complements freely. The complement of an F-head must form an extended projection with the F-head and structure above it, otherwise there is no possibility that the complement can satisfy (10). The explanation depends on the idea that the relationship between L-heads and their complements is fundamentally different from the relationship between F-heads and their complements. The relationship between a lexical head and its complement is one of semantic role assignment, such as theta-marking; that between a functional head and its complement is not. Explaining why functional and lexical heads have such different complement taking properties is the

---

[9]This definition is simplified from earlier versions, which were unnecessarily disjunctive: "every maximal projection must receive a role or be part of an extended projection which receives a role."

first piece of evidence in favor of Extended Projection – the hypothesis that complements to functional heads form a syntactic unit with the projection above them.

Further consideration of the cases in (9) clarifies some issues in the definition of an (extended) projection given in (3) and (4). Let us eliminate from (9) all the combinations that involve category mis-matches and focus on those where only F-value is at stake. We find that there are two distinguishable sub-types. The structures in (11) involve a head with a lower F-value taking a complement with a higher F-value. (For example, I is F1 and CP is F2, in the simple analysis presented above.) These are excluded by (4), in either version, since neither version allows for a lower F-value to occur higher in the extended projection.

(11)   I-CP, D-PP

The cases in (12), however, distinguish between the two alternative formulations:

(12)   I-IP, D-DP

The second version of (4), but not the first, allows a head to form an extended projection with a complement of the same functional level, since it requires only that F-value *not increase* as we descend through the extended projection, allowing for the case where F-value remains the same.[10] (van Riemsdijk's "No Value Reversal" principle (van Riemsdijk 1998: 25), which disallows a negative specification for a feature on top of a positive specification for a feature within a projection, also allows repetitions like those in (12).)

So if the structures in (12), involving an F-head taking a complement with the same F-value, are impossible, the version of the definition which requires a node lower in the extended projection to have a lower F-value than the phrase above it must be correct. If they are possible, the no-increase alternative must be correct, so that a node lower in the extended projection can have the same F-value as a higher phrase in the same extended projection.

Combinations like the one in (13), containing two identical functional projections, are probably impossible, but they are ruled out independently by economy of structure (see Grimshaw 2001, 2003), so they do not motivate an increasing F-value requirement.

(13)   [$_{CP}$ *that* [$_{CP}$ *that* IP]]

---

[10]Note that if the higher and lower heads have the same F-value, the theory will not regulate their relationship, so in principle either one can take the other as a complement. More elaborate possibilities might allow an L-head to take an LP complement but disallow a functional head with a complement of the same F-value.

While combinations of P and a PP complement have been recognized since Jackendoff 1973, the bearing of these cases on the definition of an extended projection depends on the analysis of the complement-taking P; whether it is lexical or functional, and if it is functional, what its F-value is. The properties of complementizers and prepositions are further analyzed in Section 1.4.6.

Similar issues arise where the higher head is lexical rather than functional. The no-increase definition allows the combinations V-VP and N-NP, but not N-VP or V-NP, to form single extended projections. Within the verbal system there are a number of potential cases of V-VP, where the hypothesis that they form a single extended projection seems likely to be correct. One is the V-VP structure required for a L-head with more than two arguments in Larson's (1988) analysis. In this analysis, the higher V position is filled by raising the lower V into it, so in a sense only one L-head is involved in the structure. The vP proposal of Kratzer 1996 and related work raises a similar issue: presumably the vP and the VP form a single extended projection, but the head of vP may be lexical, since it introduces the external argument. Auxiliary verbs are another potential testing ground, if they are analyzed as Vs (i.e. lexical heads) with VP complements (see Guéron and Hoekstra 1988 on auxiliaries and "verbal projections," and Rivero 2000 for arguments that some Czech auxiliaries are lexical and some functional).

A particularly interesting case which might bear on the precise F-value requirements of projection has been identified by Vos (1999) and van Riemsdijk (1998). They develop an analysis of Dutch and German measure phrases which employs lexical and functional or "semi-lexical" nouns. The hypothesis is that in the direct partitive construction, exemplified by Dutch *een plak kaas* "a piece (of) cheese," there is a single projection containing two nouns: *plak* "piece" and *kaas* "cheese."[11] Vos and van Riemsdijk argue that the first N is semi-lexical, the second lexical. English does not have the direct partitive structure. My own inves-

---

[11]Apparently both Vos and van Riemsdijk conclude that this phenomenon is inconsistent with the principles of Extended Projection, as formulated here and in earlier versions, and support the notion of a projection developed in van Riemsdijk (1990, 1998). However, the logic of this is not clear to me. The two nouns can form part of a single extended projection, provided that the measure noun has an F-value greater than that of a regular noun, if we adopt the first formulation in (4) or the definition given in Grimshaw 1991, the original version of this paper. If we adopt the second formulation, the F-value of the measure noun must be greater than or identical to that of a regular noun. The second solution sheds light on the substantive question of why both elements seem to be "nouns," i.e. to share significant properties, which is not obvious under the Vos/van Riemsdijk analysis.

tigation of English partitives (*a box/pound/pile of (the) apples*) shows that they behave like two extended projections, one headed by the measure noun and one by the lower noun (Grimshaw in prep., Schwarzschild 2002). Along similar lines, Giusti 1997: 116 states: "Quantitative adjectives are certainly lexical heads, probably with their own functional extended projection. . . ." I conclude that the no-increase version of (4) offers a number of attractive analytical possibilities. We will encounter more evidence supporting this definition of an extended projection in Section 1.4.6.

How many values does the F feature have? The answer is a large number if the conclusions of Cinque (1999) are correct. However, the theory of Extended Projection never depends on the absolute F-value of a head/projection, only on its F-value relative to that of other nodes of the same syntactic category. Thus we can proceed without fixing the upper limit. Additional projections, such as the clause internal projections TP, AgrP, and NegP of recent research (Laka 1990, Pollock 1989, Zanuttini 1990, 1997, Haegeman 1995, Bobaljik and Jonas 1996) are simply members of the verbal extended projection with the same category features as V and whatever F-values turn out to be appropriate. The inclusion of further projections poses no particular challenge to the basic tenets of the theory. Nevertheless, substantive issues of considerable interest arise in connection with functional heads and projections which (at least) appear to be optional; this will become clear when we look at the relationship between Extended Projection and selection (Section 1.6), and we will return to the analysis of NegP in particular there.

In sum, Extended Projection does not impose any principled limit on the value of F, although there is such a limit imposed by substantive principles of UG governing functional systems; see Section 1.5. It seems obvious that there is a high degree of predictability in the organization of extended projections. The F-value of a head is (at least partly) determined by the functional information that the head encodes. There are two possible outcomes. One is that F-values will prove to be highly correlated with semantic properties, but not eliminable. This appears to be the situation for other syntactic constructs, such as category labels. The fact that *dog* is a noun and *walk* a verb is highly predictable, but this does not mean that we can dispense with the role of "noun" and "verb" in the theory. (See Grimshaw 1981, included here as Chapter 3.) The other possibility is that F-value will prove to be completely redundant and the fact that only certain combinations form extended projections will follow directly from semantic theory, with no crosslinguistic variation. In this case there would ultimately be no role for

F-values in theory and all would be explained. Zwarts 1992 and Section 1.5 address some of these issues.

Extended Projection distinguishes among three kinds of head-complement relations. L-heads and their complements do not constitute extended projections but are legitimate because of theta-marking. F-heads and their complements are legitimate if and only if they form extended projections. Other combinations of F-head and complement are ruled out by this proposal, although some have been suggested in the literature. These form the topic of Section 1.4.5 and 1.4.6.

1.4 Projection and Locality

One fundamental difference between the functional-head hypothesis and the lexical-head hypothesis lies in which head is predicted to determine properties of the entire phrase. If the DP is a projection of D, then D and not N determines properties of the entire phrase; properties of the N in (14) project only to the top of NP, through the boxed nodes, and not to the top of DP.

(14)

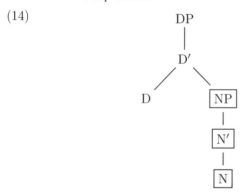

In contrast, the prediction of lexical-head theory is that the N is the head of, and determines properties of, the entire phrase. This poses a rather general locality problem for the functional head hypothesis. A verb which is locally related to its object noun under lexical-head theory is in a non-local relationship with its object under functional-head theory, in which a DP intervenes between the projection of N and the V.

Locality problems of this kind have been noted many times in the literature. For instance, Chomsky (1986a: 13–14) suggests a redefinition of "sister," which we might call "extended sister," under which VP and the subject are sisters despite the fact that the VP is embedded in I', so the VP can locally theta-mark the subject[12]. Chomsky's suggestion for the definition of (extended) sister is telling: two elements are sisters if they are "dominated by the same lexical projections." Under Extended Projection, it is easy to make sense of this. Phrases which are dominated by the same lexical projections are exactly those that are in a single extended projection. The specifier of IP and the VP node are dominated by the same lexical nodes if and only if they are in the same extended projection, thus we might say that theta-marking within a single extended projection is local.

Functional head theory is challenged whenever properties of N seem to be projected up to DP, or V to IP, and such instances suggest that the original assumption, that N is the head of DP and V is the head of IP, in fact has some force. Extended Projection offers a solution to this problem which makes it possible to maintain both the advantages of the functional head analysis and the advantages of the lexical head analysis.

The defining property of an X-bar projection is that it is the domain through which information flows from head to head. The defining property of a head is that it determines properties of the phrase that it is the head of. This follows from the theory of *projection*, in which properties of heads project, or percolate, up the tree to the entire phrase. Without Extended Projection, properties of the lexical head N or V project to NP or VP, properties of the functional head D or I to DP or IP, but properties of the lexical head do not project to the DP or IP. If the only kind of projection is a perfect one, it follows that the relationship between the lexical head N or V, and any element outside NP or VP, is non-local. This is problematic for phenomena which are in general taken to be local, such as selection and agreement. Either we give up on the locality restriction, allowing many unattested relationships, or we stipulate that maximal projections do not count for locality in just these cases.

Under Extended Projection, however, there is a principled solution to this problem. Both the lexical phrase and the functional phrase are projections of the lexical head. In extended projections, like perfect projections, properties of the head(s) project through the head-structure, just as categorial information does. Thus, information about the lexical head projects automatically through the lexical projection and through the functional extended projection. DP and PP are projections of N, and IP and CP are projections of V. (See Section 1.4.6 on the relation-

---

[12]This assumes that the subject is theta-marked in specifier of IP position, rather than VP-internally.

ship of PP to NP, and CP to VP.) Properties of N thus project to DP and PP, while properties of V project to IP and CP. In this sense, NP under DP and DP under PP are *transparent*, and so are VP under IP and IP under CP. This is because they form parts of larger projections of their heads. The only *transparent* maximal projections are those that fall within an extended projection. An IP or DP complement to a V, for example, is not transparent, since it does not form an extended projection with the VP.

An immediate consequence is that certain key relationships which are otherwise non-local become local under Extended Projection. I will examine here several such cases, involving semantic selection and agreement.

1.4.1 Semantic Selection

If the D is the head of the DP, a verb cannot locally select for properties of its object NP such as animacy or plurality because the complement of the verb is the DP, and N is not the head of DP. Such selection is nevertheless possible:[13]

(15)   a.   They merged the files/*the file.

     b.   They amalgamated the files/*the file.

     c.   They combined the files/*the file.

Under Extended Projection, the selectional relationship is local. Since both the N and the D are heads of the DP, their properties are all projected to the DP, and available for selection by V. This solution is possible only if the N counts as a head of DP, and the NP and DP projections form a single extended projection.

A note of clarification: Extended Projection explains which configurations admit selection in principle. The issue of what can select and what can be selected for is not only a matter of projection though. It depends also on the theory of selection, which characterizes what properties can be selected for by what types of heads. Thus the fact that definiteness does not generally seem to be selectable, while plurality is, for example, to be explained by the theory of selection and not by the theory of configurational representation and projection. What can be selected for in any given case is the result of the theory of selection determining what information is selectable in principle, interacting with the theory of projection, and determining what information is configurationally available for selection. The further implications of Extended Projection for selection will be examined in Section 1.6.

---

[13]Grimshaw 1993, included here as Chapter 2, distinguishes between true semantic selection and real world incompatibility.

The fact that selection is problematic for functional head theory was recognized in Abney (1987), where it is proposed that the NP/DP combination forms a "semantic projection" or "s-projection." It forms, in other words, a projection for semantic relations. However, the problem is more general, involving not just semantic relations but syntactic ones, including the case of number agreement to be addressed next. Hence, the solution must also be more general.

1.4.2 Agreement

Agreement is another typically local phenomenon, but again we find apparent violations of locality which can be resolved under Extended Projection. If information projects from all of the heads of an extended projection, we expect consistency within a projection for all projected features. Projected features must agree throughout the extended projection (PP-DP-NP and CP-IP-VP), and wherever morphology records the value of these features they will be visible. Between extended projections, we expect no constraints to hold, or at least none that are attributable to projection. Thus the existence of apparent locality violations within extended projections, and only within extended projections, provides an important source of evidence for the theory.

Number agreement for subjects exemplifies the phenomenon. As (16) shows, a verb agrees with the number of its subject even when that number is marked on the N, and not on the D:

(16) a. the dogs are   *the dogs is
      b. the dog is   *the dog are
      c. dogs are   *dogs is

Under Extended Projection, the agreement is local, despite appearances. The N is [+plural] by virtue of its morphology, hence the entire DP is [+plural] by Extended Projection, and the verb or Infl agrees with the DP, by local specifier-head agreement. In contrast, the relationship is non-local under standard projection, since the verb or Infl and NP are separated by a maximal projection (DP).

The extended projection analysis automatically requires "agreement" between a functional head which is specified for number and the head noun of its complement. For *a* and *this/these/that/those*, assuming these to be F-heads, the features projected from D to DP will include number, and the features projected from N to NP to DP will also include number. A *consistency* requirement will therefore automatically exclude cases where the D and the N disagree in number, allowing only combinations where both have the same value for the feature, or at least one of the two is unspecified for the feature. The functional head and the lexical head of the extended projection can never have contradictory values for projected properties, because both sets of features are projected onto the same phrase. Thus the behavior of Ds that do encode number follows from same principles as behavior of Ds, like *the*, that do not encode number.

There are some other possible solutions to the locality problem which must be touched on. It is tempting to treat the plural as a determiner, making it the head of DP and hence making its properties locally available to I. However, this is not a workable solution, since the plural can cooccur with a determiner in phrases like *the dogs*.

An important class of alternative solutions requires encoding the number on the determiner in one way or another. For example, it is possible to treat *the* as ambiguously singular and plural, and have it *agree* with its complement in number by head-complement agreement, or perhaps more plausibly have it *select* the number of its complement. This treats *the* as covertly encoding number, as some determiners do overtly. Such a solution is workable, but requires positing two versions of *the*, claiming in effect that we are just observing accidental properties of *the* rather than any principled phenomenon. If positing functional structure over lexical structure requires such analyses in a substantial number of cases, this suggests that there is something systematic and more interesting than stipulated lexical ambiguity involved.

The same technique can be appealed to in a solution to the non-local semantic selection problem of Section 1.4.1. Multiple cases of *the* could be posited, one each for (semantically) singular and plural animates, one each for (semantically) singular and plural inanimates and so forth. It seems hardly necessary to argue that this is not an insightful solution.

An alternative which at first sight seems more promising would exploit under-specification of a kind. Suppose we hypothesize that when D is not specified for some feature, such as $[+/-\text{plural}]$, then the value of the complement can project. A head like *the* could then be unspecified for plurality, and the NP would determine the plurality of the DP. This solution differs from those suggested above for semantic selection and number agreement, in that a feature specification projects through the extended projection only if the functional head is not marked for a value of the feature. Above we assumed that feature specifications always project. One piece of evidence that they should always project is that this allows us to explain the behavior of agreeing determiners as we saw above. In the case of a plural noun and a singular determiner, for example, the value of the number feature for the noun must project, even though the determiner is also specified for number, if the ill-formedness of the combination is to be explained by projection.

More importantly, however, it seems that the percolation of unspecified information must itself be embedded within a theory of Extended Projection. A V is not specified for number, but the VP does not inherit number from a DP complement to V. When, then, does inheritance occur? The answer that must be given is essentially: within an extended projection. By this reasoning, then, percolation of unspecified information is not an alternative to Extended Projection, but an alternative formulation of the percolation mechanism to be used within Extended Projection.

Within the verbal extended projection we find evidence identical in structure to the cases we have already seen. Relations within an extended projection can span maximal projections. Outside extended projections (i.e. between them) these same relations do not cross maximal projections.

Consider the relationship between a higher V, a C, and I. The question at issue is how to characterize the dependencies illustrated in (17).

(17)   a.   We arranged for him to leave at 6. (*left)

   b.   We thought that he left at 6. (*to leave)

At first glance, it appears that the relationship between V, I and C can be viewed as a local head-to-head relationship, as in Baltin 1989. The verb *arrange* might select *for*, while *for* selects *to*. The verb *think* might select *that*, while *that* selects [+tense]. This solution works fine for examples like (17). The problem is that examples like (18) do not fit in with this account: here the relationship extends across the C *that*.

(18)   a.   We requested **that** he leave/?left at 6.

   b.   We thought **that** he left/*leave at 6.

The verb *request* selects a subjunctive (more or less obligatorily), while *think* does not allow a subjunctive. These selectional requirements are enforced even though the same complementizer is used for the indicative and the subjunctive.

The problem here is analogous to the problem of the determiner *the* in number agreement, analyzed above. Just as *the* fails to encode number which projects up from NP, *that* does not encode the indicative/subjunctive distinction, yet this distinction is available at the CP level. As before, there are basically two solutions. We could posit two different cases of *that*, one subjunctive and one indicative, and proceed as before. (See Laka 1990 for a version of this solution.) However, under Extended Projection the solution is already in place. The mood distinction is encoded on I, I is the head of IP, and IP forms an extended projection with CP. Hence the feature will project all the way to the CP node, where it can be locally selected by a verb.[14]

The complementizer *for* is positively specified for whatever feature infinitives have, as is *to*, whereas *that* and the tense morphemes are negatively specified for infinitival features, hence they will never occur with *to*. The complementizer *that* is specified as non-infinitival, but unspecified for the subjunctive-indicative distinction. Hence it will occur in both moods. The only requirement is that all projected features agree, and this is what governs the permissible combinations. The mood of the entire CP is determined by the mood of the IP via projection, regardless of whether *that* is specified for mood or not. This is, then, another case of projected agreement. The crucial assumption is that CP is a projection of IP. Otherwise (locality of) the relationship cannot be maintained.

In principle we expect that a complementizer can show overt agreement with a phrase in the right relationship to it, namely a specifier of one of the heads of CP. This occurs in certain Germanic languages, where the complementizer inflects for the number or person of the subject DP (Bennis and Haegeman 1984, Bayer 1984, Kathol 2000).

(19)   West Flemish (Haegeman 1991: 530)

   a. ...da Jan noa Gent goat.
      "...that Jan to Ghent goes"

   b. ...dan Jan en Pol noa Gent goan.
      "...that Jan and Pol to Ghent go"

The analysis of this is straightforward: the complementizer has more than one morphological form, which simply reflects the normal (silent in English) agreement pattern. The subject is in specifier of IP, and agrees with I by specifier-head agreement. Properties of I project to IP, and from IP to CP by Extended Projection. Thus the CP in the first example in (19) is [−plural], in the second it is [+plural]. The head C is marked for the same information: *da* being [−plural] and *dan* [+plural]. Properties of C project to CP by normal projection, so both the number of the complementizer and the number of Spec of IP are

---

[14]Baltin 1989 argues in favor of head to head selection on the basis of wh complements. He argues that since the +wh complementizer occurs with both finite and non-finite clauses, any predicate which selects a +wh complementizer must necessarily occur with both finite and non-finite wh complements: *I know what they did/I know what to do*. There is a complication with this argument, because there are in fact predicates which occur with finite wh complements but not infinitival ones, contra Baltin's assumptions: *Our decision depends on when/whether the train leaves/*Our decision depends on when/whether to leave*. The theory of selection proposed in Section 1.6 will not allow any predicate to select for finiteness, so the contrast with *depend on* must be due to the semantics of the complement.

registered on CP, and they will have to agree. Hence *da* will have to occur when the subject is [−plural], and when the subject is [+plural] the form will be *dan*.[15]

By this reasoning, apparently non-local agreement is actually local, confined to an extended projection (though see Finer 1997 for a problematic case where a C seems to agree with a superordinate subject). Hence a C can agree in number with Spec of IP, but a V should not be able to agree in number with the subject of its subordinate clause. It is noteworthy that in one recent study of feature percolation it is stipulated that there is no percolation from complements of lexical categories (Cole, Hermon and Sung 1993). This is exactly the situation that Extended Projection predicts.

A fascinating case of non-local agreement has been discovered in Korean (Song 1988, Kim 1994). When the subject of a clause is plural, "spurious" plural markers can appear in several places in the clause, as illustrated by (20) (taken from Kim 1994: 303).

(20) ai-**tul**-i   sensayngnim-kkey-**tul**   yelsimhi-**tul**
     child-PLU-NOM   teacher-DAT-PLU   intently-PLU

     cilmun-ul   ha-ko-**tul**   iss-ta.
     question-ACC   do-COMP-PLU   be

     "The children are asking questions to the teacher intently"

The plural markers, bolded in (20), occur not only after the plural subject, but also after the indirect object (which is singular), the adverb, and the complementizer marking the edge of the subordinate clause.

The spreading of the plural marker can be explained as follows: the Spec of IP is plural, making I plural. Since I and IP form an extended projection with the CP, the CP is plural by projection, and its head can thus be plural marked. Assuming that the NP is a complement to the verb *ha-*, and the PP and Adverb are in specifier positions of VP projections, downward projection of the plural feature from I will allow them to be plural marked as well. I refer the reader to the references cited for further analysis, but there is one important prediction to be noted here. If the spreading of the plural marker is indeed a function of feature projection through an extended projection, the phenomenon should be clause bounded; i.e. the plural feature should not spread into a lower or higher extended projection. Kim (1994) argues that these plurals are subject to a "Coargument Condition," citing the ungram-

---

[15]In this proposal no role is played by a functional Agr head, although there is no fundamental incompatibility with positing one. See Belletti 2001 for a review of research on Agr.

maticality of (21), in which a plural marker occurs on the locative in
the subordinate clause, marked by square brackets, and the potentially
triggering plural is in the higher clause. The plural marker on the locative is perfectly grammatical if the subject of the subordinate clause is
plural, as Kim demonstrates.

(21) sensayngnim-**tul**-un   [Kim-i   emma-lul
      teacher-PLU-TOP   Kim-NOM   mother-ACC

      hakkyo-ey(*-**tul**)   mosie-olila-ko-**tul**]
      school-LOC(*-PLU)   bring-COMP-PLU

      sayngkak hayessta.
      thought

> "Teachers thought that Kim would bring his mother to the school"

Several colleagues have raised the issue of what I will call "over-
agreement" predicted by the present theory. Assuming that there is
general specifier head agreement and projection of features throughout
the extended projection, two kinds of over-agreement may occur.

First, the entire extended projection will be marked for all features
of specifiers within it. For example, if a specifier is singular/plural,
the entire extended projection is singular/plural. When the extended
projection is IP, CP, or PP, this makes the prediction that it will in
turn induce agreement. So, for example, a PP with a plural noun as
its extended head or a CP with a plural subject should induce plural
agreement if they themselves occur as specifiers. Possible cases would
be CP subjects (but see Koster 1978) and PPs in locative inversion
structures (see Bresnan and Mchombo 1987). To at least some extent,
this is a problem for all theories of projection, not just Extended Projection. Why doesn't the West Flemish CP with a plural head trigger
plural number agreement on a verb? In fact, why don't a noun and
a possessive DP specifier have to agree in number, by specifier head
agreement?

The second case of over-agreement is clearly problematic for the theory of Extended Projection. If every specifier in an extended projection
agrees with its head, and all heads agree with each other, it follows that
all specifiers will have to agree. This rules out many obviously possible
structures, such as a plural wh phrase in specifier of CP and a singular
subject in specifier of IP; a −wh specifier in IP and a +wh specifier in
CP; a singular subject and a plural object in Icelandic transitive exple-
tives (Bobaljik and Jonas 1996). Also, an unmoved wh phrase in spec
of IP will make CP +wh, so that sentences like *Who thought (that) who
was a fool?* will violate the selection of *think*. Within an extended pro-

jection, the head of any projection should be able to show agreement with the specifier of any other projection.

The problem is to rein in the over-agreement predictions while allowing for the attested non-local agreements: the agreeing complementizer and Korean plural phenomenon and others discussed in the text. A number of factors affect the exact predictions made for agreement: what is truly a specifier; the feature characteristics of the various heads of the extended projection and principles governing features, such as requirements of identity or consistency; whether features project to a higher node only if the higher node has no independent specification. Grosu (1996: 290) proposes that features that are inherent to an individual extended projection block percolation of features that are inherited from another, e.g. by specifier-head agreement.

1.4.3 Wh phrases and Projection

The behavior of wh phrases provides evidence that PP participates in the same extended projection as NP, i.e. for the claim that PP-DP-NP form an extended projection: the feature +wh projects through the transparent DP to a dominating PP, whereas it never projects through a dominating VP or NP because they are not transparent as they do not form extended projections with their complements.

When a wh NP/DP is dominated by a PP and fronting occurs, whether in a relative or in an interrogative, the dominating PP can move instead of the wh NP/DP (Ross's (1967) "pied-piping;" see van Riemsdijk 1985, Cowper 1987, Cole, Hermon and Sung 1993). Thus we find the alternatives in (22):

(22) a. The stone which they found a note under...

     b. Which stone did they find a note under?

     c. The stone under which they found a note...

     d. Under which stone did they find a note?

     e. The woman who they gave the job to ...

     f. Who did they give the job to?

     g. The woman to whom they gave the job ...

     h. To whom did they give the job?

Why can the entire PP front? The critical hypothesis here is that only a [+wh] phrase can undergo movement in a restrictive relative or wh complement.[16] It follows from positing an extended nominal projection including PP that if the D (or the N) is +wh, this feature will project to PP. Hence the PP will be [+wh], and eligible for movement; it is just as much a wh phrase as the DP. Thus, to think of pied-piping as the dragging along of a preposition is really misleading – the movement is a reflection of the fact that the prepositional phrase is part of the same extended projection as the wh-marked element and hence is indirectly a wh phrase itself.[17] There is an affinity between this explanation for pied-piping and the one given by Ross (1967), who suggested that PPs move because they are really just a special kind of NP. Under Extended Projection, PPs are indeed a kind of nominal – the biggest kind there is.

Crucially, the wh feature will never be passed on to a verbal projection, such as V′ dominating a [+wh] DP or a [+wh] PP, since the verbal projection will never form an extended projection with the nominal element for reasons already discussed. So the apparently idiosyncratic fact that only P seems to pied-pipe is explained: PP is the category that forms an extended projection with a DP complement, it is DPs that are potentially +wh, and hence it is PPs that can inherit the +wh feature by agreement. In the very same structural configuration, namely a +wh DP as a complement to a head, the head pied-pipes if it is a P, and does not pied-pipe if it is a V, just as Extended Projection predicts.

---

[16]It is critical to distinguish between fronting in an interrogative or restrictive relative from fronting in an appositive relative. In appositives, a wide range of phrases can be fronted provided that they contain a wh pronoun:

(i) This topic, a book about which was published today, ...

(ii) This topic, to talk about which is always lots of fun, ...

In contrast, restrictions on pied-piping in interrogatives and restrictive relatives are extremely tight. See Cowper 1987 for discussion and analysis and van Riemsdijk 1985 on pied-piping of clauses in German.

[17]Less clear, under this reasoning, is why the preposition does not always front with the DP, i.e. why it can be stranded in English. One possibility is that the wh feature optionally projects to the PP, and that the DP moves alone when the PP is not +wh. Alternatively the feature may always project to the PP, and the principles governing movement may simply allow *any* wh phrase to move, not just the largest. Note that this would not allow NP to move stranding D, or AP to move stranding Deg, since the wh feature is located on D and Deg, so NP and AP do not qualify as wh phrases, provided that the wh feature cannot project downward onto NP and AP.

Provided that the +wh feature can project appropriately, phrases of arbitrary complexity can undergo movement in interrogatives and restrictive relatives:[18]

(23) a. I wonder which book they read.

b. I wonder whose book they read.

c. I wonder whose mother's friend's book they read.

(23) illustrates the cases where the wh element is the head of the specifier of a fronted DP, or even the head of the specifier of the specifier of the specifier of the fronted DP, as in the final example, which is analyzed in (24). These examples are perfectly well-formed, not a surprise if the wh feature on the head of the specifier DP makes the DP +wh, and specifier-head agreement makes the dominating DP +wh. This DP participates in specifier-head agreement in turn, and so the wh head can be embedded arbitrarily deeply inside the specifier.

(24)

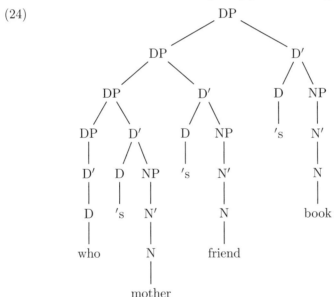

In order to have the feature specification +wh, a phrase must inherit the wh feature either from its specifier position, or from its head. When

---

[18] J. Rooryck (p.c.) asks why *right* and a PP do not combine to form wh phrases. If they do not, I have no explanation. In restrictive relatives they seem relatively acceptable, less so in interrogatives.

(i) (?Right) underneath which tree did they say we'd find the treasure?

(ii) The book (right) behind which the bible stands ...

the wh element is in the complement of a lexical head, the entire phrase does not count as a wh phrase, as (25) and (26) show.[19]

(25) a. *I wonder **a book about who(m)** they read.

 b. I wonder who they read a book about.

(26) a. *I wonder **very proud of who(m)** they are.

 b. I wonder how proud of him they are.

This is because features do not project to the head from the complement of N in (25), or from the complement of A in (26). Extended Projection predicts that features project from a complement only within an extended projection, as in the case of PPs.[20]

In sum, in order for a phrase to count as a wh phrase, it must either have a wh head or a wh specifier. In just one case, having a wh complement is enough to make the phrase +wh, and that is in the case of prepositional phrases. PPs are the only structures which form extended projections with a +wh DP, and hence the only structures which can inherit +wh from their complement.

1.4.4 Extended Projection and Head Movement

Head-to-head movement is extremely well established between V, I and C, and other heads occurring between them (see especially Koopman 1984, Pollock 1989 and subsequent work, and further references below). Similarly, there is substantial evidence for head-movement of N to D and to positions between them (Abney 1987, Ritter 1987, 1991, Cinque 1994, Longobardi 1994). The examples in (27), taken from Haegemann 1991, illustrate the much-studied phenomenon of verb second in German, in which a V raises to I, and I raises to C (den Besten 1977).

(27) a. ...daß Karl das Buch kauft.
  that Karl the book buys
  "that Karl buys the book."

---

[19]Here again it is crucial to separate appositive relatives from restrictives and interrogatives. For example, the wh-fronting in (25a) is ungrammatical in a restrictive relative: *Any man a book about who(m) you have read ..., but comparatively acceptable at least in a non-restrictive: That man, a book about who(m) you have read ...

[20]Samek-Lodovici points out (p.c.) that what counts as a negative phrase which can prepose in English inversion structures is governed by the same principles, as we expect. We find PPs with negative D extended heads fronting, but not NPs with negative Ds heading their PP complements: Under no circumstances will he be appointed; No books about that topic will they ever assign, *Books on no controversial topics will they ever assign. The first two have the slightly pompous and marginal status that these examples generally have in English, the last one is simply impossible. See Bayer 1996 for the same idea applied to Q features on quantifiers.

    b. Karl kauft das Buch.
        "Karl buys the book"

    c. Gestern   kaufte Karl dieses Buch.
        yesterday bought Karl this   book
        "Yesterday Karl bought this book"

Zanuttini's analysis of negation posits a C^0 which must be filled, or
have its feature checked; she points out that the elements that can satisfy the requirement are verbs, verbal features, the preverbal negative
marker, and the complementizer; in other words, the heads of the verbal
extended projection (Zanuttini 1997: 142).

    It is immediately striking that all of these cases of X-zero movement
are *within an extended projection*. When V raises to I and the resulting
complex raises to C, for example, movement is between the heads of a
single verbal extended projection. The same holds for raising from N
to D (and to P), illustrated in (28).

(28)

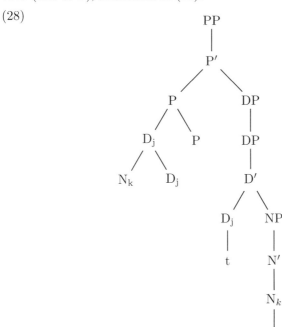

In contrast, consider lexical heads with their potential complements:

(29) a.   V-CP; V-IP; V-VP; V-PP; V-DP; V-NP

       b.   N-CP; N-IP; N-VP; N-PP; N-DP; N-NP

The examples of (29) are head-complement combinations which do not form extended projections, with the possible exception of lexical heads with lexical projections as complements (Section 1.3). Presumably some of these are ruled out by principles other than projection licensing, e.g. it may not be possible for an NP with no DP over it to occur as a complement to a lexical head in the first place, but let us set that question aside. The point is that every one of this set of head-complement relations represents a potential case of head-raising, in which a head inside one extended projection moves to a head position in another extended projection.

The empirical generalization appears to be that local incorporation of N, V, or P into a verb, as in Baker 1988, is indeed possible (presumably supporting the view that prepositions can be lexical as well as functional, see Section 1.4.6). What seems to be impossible is movement of a head from the lower extended projection *through the higher extended projection*. For example, we do not find functional heads raising from the lower projection to the higher. Nor do we find the lexical head of the lower projection raising to a functional position in the higher projection. This provides further support for the extended projection hypothesis: extended projections are the domain for head raising.[21]

Li (1990) makes a proposal which addresses the restricted nature of head movement. Observing that head movement from, for example, V to I to V to I is never found, but is allowed by the theory as it stands, Li proposes generalizing the idea of improper movement to this case. If the V is taken to be an A position and the I an A-bar position, then movement from A to $\bar{\text{A}}$ will be allowed but movement from $\bar{\text{A}}$ to A can be eliminated for head movement on the same grounds as improper movement for maximal projections. We need a more general formulation of Li's proposal in order to accommodate additional heads; such a formulation could simply be phrased in terms of F-values, and could require that a head can move only into a position with a higher F-value, or perhaps only to a position with an F-value that is not lower than that of the head itself. If we choose the latter formulation, lexical heads will be allowed to raise to other lexical heads, accommodating the head-movement analyses of Baker 1988[22]. (Note that Li's proposal similarly allows movement from one A-position to another, hence from one lexical head to another).

In sum, I have suggested that head movement is limited to extended projections. One consequence of this is that a strict categorial relation-

---

[21]Though see Baker and Hale 1990, especially their note 1, for fuller discussion.

[22]Other analyses of these phenomena, such as that in Rosen 1989, treat them as lexical, rather than syntactic in nature.

ship is always maintained between the moving head and the head it adjoins to; verbs raise to positions in the verbal extended projection, nouns to positions in the nominal extended projection and so forth. Standing back a little, it is no surprise that head movement should be limited in this way. Extended projections are structures which organize the information pertaining to a particular (lexical) head and its projection.

1.4.5 Category Neutrality and Apparently Mixed Extended Projections

As pointed out in Section 1.3, the Generalized Theta Criterion plus the definition of extended projection eliminate combinations like D with a VP complement, I with an NP complement and P with an IP complement, since the complements are neither complements to lexical heads nor part of extended projections. While most of the combinations ruled out by the theory are indeed unattested, some have been proposed as analyses of various constructions, including gerunds (Abney 1987), psychological predicates (Georgopoulos 1987), copula constructions (Chung 1990, Doherty 1996, 1997) and the complements to determiners studied in Zaring and Hirschbühler 1997, and Borsley and Kornfilt 2000. Each of these studies has proposed, in one variant or another, that a functional head can take a complement which, in the analysis of categories given here, it does not match in category.

In such cases, the theory suggests a couple of possible solutions. One possibility is that the constructions involve lexical heads with complements, not a single extended projection. The other possibility, which I pursue here, is that these combinations do form single extended projections, but their categorial description is not exactly as the earlier characterizations have assumed. Since a category mis-match will prevent a head and complement from forming an extended projection, the argument I will make here is that there is no category mis-match in these cases. These apparently illegitimate combinations are exactly those where either the *head* or the *complement* is not in reality a member of the category that it appears to belong to.

Instead, these heads and/or complements are *neutral* between (at least) two categories. Thus they will form an extended projection with elements of more than one category, provided that they meet the requirements in all other respects. If the head is neutral between two categories and the complement belongs to one of these two, then an extended projection is formed. If the complement is neutral between two categories and the head belongs to one of them, an extended projection will again be formed.

The exact set of possible neutralizations depends heavily on the theory of syntactic categories. (The apparent naturalness of N/V neutrality clearly supports a theory of features in which N and V are highly similar, such as that of Jackendoff 1977 for example.) Let us assume that neutrality for some category distinction is represented by lack of specification for a feature. Suppose, for example, that N is [+nominal] and V is [−nominal]. An element can be V/N neutral if it simply lacks a specification for [nominal]. Of course, under Extended Projection the neutralizability of N and V holds equally for D and I, P and C, since these are categorially the same as N and V. What is important, and expected under the requirements of Extended Projection, is that apparently mixed projections are possible only where the head has an ambiguous category status, and not for the clear-cut instances involving uncontroversial nouns and verbs, for example. This supports the claim that these structures have to form extended projections and that extended projections must satisfy category matching, contra the conclusions of Borsley and Kornfilt 2000.

If apparently mixed projections must form extended projections, we also predict that they must conform to Extended Projection with respect to F-value. Thus we expect to find, in principle, $F2$ heads with $F1$ complements or $F1$ heads with $F0$ complements, but we should never find an $F1$ head with an $F2$ complement, and so on. In contrast, under the standard theory of projection, which posits only perfect projections, no particular predictions are made about what combinations can look like, either with respect to syntactic category, or with respect to functional level; any combinations should be permissible. This is because standard projection theory does not analyze complex structures as *projections* at all, but only as combinations of independent projections. Hence there is no reason to expect any particular relationship to hold between the functional status or category of the higher head and the category of the complement.

Abney (1987) proposes an analysis of the category switching effect observed in English "verbal" gerunds, such as those in (30).

(30)   a.   *Their studying this problem* will not be useful.

   b.   I resent *Mary's eating cookies* in front of me.

These gerunds have the external distribution of DPs, and their subjects appear as possessives. Nevertheless they have the internal structure of VPs, taking adverbials and not adjectives as modifiers, and assigning case like verbs do.

Abney's proposal is that a gerund should be analyzed as a VP complement to D, approximately as in (31).

(31)

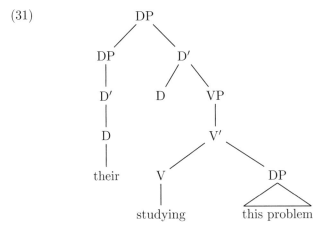

The fundamental argument for this solution is extremely convincing. It makes it possible to characterize the point at which nominal properties change to verbal properties, and it does so without doing violence to the basic principles of X-bar theory. Moreover it predicts that the external distribution of gerunds is that of a nominal, while their internal structure is that of a verbal construction.[23]

However, since D and V are of different syntactic categories, the VP and DP cannot form an extended projection, hence the structure in (31) is not legitimate. The key here is of course the categorial hypothesis; the problem arises only under the assumption that verbal gerunds literally contain V and D. One possible solution is that the apparent "D" in these structures is really no such thing, being neutral in category (like Deg as analyzed below) or perhaps ambiguous. The status of "D" would then be responsible for the odd categorial properties of gerunds. This view is attractive in view of the fact that the typical determiners do not combine with verbal gerunds; the hypothesis would be that the true determiners in (32) are nominal and hence do not occur with verbal complements, while the apparent determiner in gerunds (whether it is 's itself, a null element, or *ing*, see Abney 1987 for discussion) is neutral.

(32)   *One/the/an eating cookies is enough to ruin anyone's diet.

---

[23]The structure in (31) cannot be correct if Cinque's arguments for functional projections as the loci of adjuncts are correct (Cinque 1994, 1999). It turns out that both nominal and verbal gerunds can contain elements from at least as high on the hierarchy as "Mood$_{evidential}$:"

(i) Mary's allegedly eating cookies upset her dietician.

(ii) Mary's alleged eating of cookies upset her dietician.

Hence by the logic of Cinque's argument, these gerunds must contain many functional projections. See Section 1.5 for further discussion of the hierarchy of functional heads.

However, this solution results in the verbal category being projected from the complement to the functional projection, which gives the wrong results, since we know that gerunds are always nominal with respect to their external distributional properties.

The other possible resolution of the clash between the category D and the category VP focuses on the status of the apparent VP. We know that in addition to verbal gerunds, there is also a nominal gerund construction which has consistently nominal properties. Nonetheless the morphology of the nominal gerund is identical to the morphology of the verbal gerund.

(33) a. Mary's constantly eating cookies is blowing her diet.

  b. Mary's constant eating of cookies is blowing her diet.

This suggests that the -*ing* head of a gerund is itself N/V neutral. Hence in a "verbal gerund," the head that dominates -*ing*, and its projections, are not really verbal; they belong to a category which is neutral between V and N. D is fully specified as nominal, and has an *F*-value higher than that of its complement, so D forms an extended projection with its complement, provided that we take the definition of extended projection to require that the categories be non-distinct rather than identical. The -*ing* complement to D does not violate the Generalized Theta Criterion, and the existence of verbal gerunds is consistent with the principles of Extended Projection.

The representation in (31) is now corrected to that in (34), where a +Nom head takes a +/−Nom complement and forms an extended projection with it.

(34)

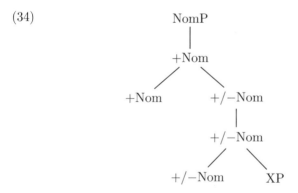

This solution to the problem posed by verbal gerunds leaves unexplained why properties cluster in just the way they do: verbal gerunds take bare DP complements and adverbial, not adjectival, modification.

Nominal gerunds take only prepositional complements and take adjectival, not adverbial, modification. The neutral *-ing* hypothesis, without further elaboration, does not explain why a $+/-$Nom structure should not simultaneously admit both complements from the +Nominal options and adjuncts from the $-$Nominal options. It is possible that adjectives occur only in phrases which are +Nominal, and adverbs elsewhere. I leave the problem open here.[24]

In sum, it seems fair to say that in the case of gerunds both the hypothesized D and the hypothesized VP have somewhat murky categorial status. While the preponderance of the evidence at present suggests that the "VP" is the source of the apparently mixed properties of gerunds, there is much that is not understood about the properties of the "D."

As D appears to take an illegitimate VP complement in gerunds, so I has been thought to take a wide variety of complements, and not just the verbal projections that Extended Projection would predict. Chung (1990) reports that in Chamorro, VP, AP, DP/NP and PP can all occur as complements to Infl, with no intervening copula. While the AP cases pattern with VPs, the N- and P-headed predicates differ from them in several ways: in word order, in morphology, and in disallowing wh-movement of the complement of their heads. These differences, Chung argues, can be attributed to independently verifiable properties of the heads concerned. Doherty (1996) shows that the Irish copula is a functional head, a kind of inflection in fact, but one which takes a variety of individual level predicates as syntactic complements: NP/DP, AP and PP. He notes (p. 36) that only nominal predicates are fully productive in the modern language. In fact, English copula *be* invites a parallel analysis. Its ability to undergo subject-auxiliary inversion separates it from the true lexical verbs, making it a functional head by that criterion. It takes PP, AP and DP complements *(She is in the house/angry/the winner)*, and possibly VP complements also, if progressive and/or passive *be* is unified with copula *be*.

These structures challenge Extended Projection as proposed here. If the copula is a functional head which combines with a variety of complements, it must be neutral between the categories the complements belong to. This would allow for the variety of complement types. The problem is that it also predicts that the category of the complement will project through the entire extended projection, making a copula

---

[24]Of course, the D-with-a-VP-complement hypothesis does not really explain this either, without a crucial stipulation. It stipulates D-VP, and if we can guarantee that any intermediate projections are verbal, we can derive the fact that only adverbs and not adjectives can modify a verbal gerund.

sentence nominal if the complement to the copula is a DP, adjectival if the complement is an AP, and so forth. There is no evidence for this effect; for example, the same predicates take copula sentences as complements regardless of the category of the complement to *be*. Copulas thus stand as a problem for Extended Projection.

A further puzzle in which a functional head takes an unexpected lexical complement is posed by degree heads. Deg heads take two kinds of complement, adjective phrase and adverbial phrase. As we have already seen, this is possible, under Extended Projection, if the functional head is neutral in category in just the right way – neutral between the categories of its complements.

Neutrality provides the answer to a problem raised by Edwin Williams (p.c.) and Rothstein (1991) in connection with the functional head hypothesis. By extension from the analysis of VP and NP, we should treat AdjP and AdvP as complements to a functional category, which should presumably be the Degree element which occurs in phrases like *so quick, so quickly*. (See Abney (1987), Corver (1990, 1991, 1997a) for a proposal of this type, and Rothstein (1991) for comments.) However, the degree system is the same for adjectives and adverbs, so the head of the functional projection must be of the same syntactic category in both cases. Hence the functional projection will always be of this category: DegP if the functional head is of the category Deg, for example. But now we predict, incorrectly of course, that the distribution of the functional category over AdvP and the functional category over AdjP will be the same, since they are of the same category. This problem is really another instance of the kind of locality problem discussed in Section 1.4.2. In this case it is categorial information, rather than information about number or meaning, that is apparently made inaccessible under the functional head hypothesis.

From the perspective of Extended Projection, these constructions pose an additional problem: the Deg element and its projection must form an extended projection with the complement AdjP or AdvP: otherwise the complement will violate the Generalized Theta Criterion. But how can the same element form an extended projection with adjectives, which require that it be of adjectival category, and with adverbs, which require that it be of adverbial category, when we know that adverbs and adjectives are of different categories?

Note that, as I pointed out with respect to the locality problems discussed in Section 1.4.2, there is always an uninteresting solution to such problems – posit two of everything. However, both of the problems are solved under Extended Projection if we posit that Deg is of a category which is neutral between adjective and adverb. The Deg and its projec-

tion will now form an extended projection with the complement AdvP
or AdjP, meeting the requirements of the Generalized Theta Criterion.
The category of the lexical head will project to the functional projection according to the usual principles by which categorial information
projects through the extended projection. Hence the entire projection
will be adjectival if its lexical head is adjectival and adverbial if its
lexical head is adverbial. The external distribution of the functional
projection will in fact depend on its lexical head, because the AdvP or
AdjP node will pass its features up to DegP.

For example, we can assign the feature analyses of Adv, Adj, and
Deg given in (35), where the feature(s) that distinguish adjectives from
adverbs are unspecified for Degree elements:

(35)   Adj   [+cat1 −cat2]
       Adv   [+cat1 +cat2]
       Deg   [+cat1]

In a phrasal configuration, the lexical head will be either [+cat1 +cat2]
or [+cat1 −cat2], and these features will percolate up to the lexical
projections, and from there to the functional projections. The functional head will always be [+cat1], and this feature will percolate up
to the functional projection. At the DegP level, therefore, the features
of Deg will be neutral between the adverbial and adjectival categories,
but the features of the lexical head will be compatible with only one of
the possible instantiations of the features of Deg, hence the functional
projection will inherit its features from the lexical head.

As in all the cases we have seen, this effect is predicted to be limited
to extended projections. Thus we predict that functional heads can be
category neutral and thus allow projection to transmit the category
of their complement to their own projection, but lexical heads will
never do this. A complement to an L-head will never form an extended
projection with the projection of the L-head, so there is no way for
categorial, or other, information to project through the complement to
the projection of the L-head.

The solution proposed here for DegPs is similar to that given in
Lefebvre and Massam (1988) for the distribution of D in Haitian Creole. They argue that D selects NP and S complements, and that the
entire DP is nominal when D takes an NP complement and sentential
when D takes a sentential complement. From this they conclude that D
inherits its categorial features from the lexical head, and more generally,
that "minor categories bear no major categorial features" p. 219, but
get their features by inheritance. In the theory of Extended Projection,
functional heads certainly do have category features in general. How-

ever, the Lefebvre and Massam analysis can be retained in essence: the head is category neutral (again between nominal and verbal) and Extended Projection does the rest. Thus the properties of the grammatical situation they were looking at are entailed by the theory of Extended Projection. The same is true for Rothstein's (1991) proposal that Deg is a functional head that projects structure but not category. Extended Projection provides a general system within which this proposal finds its place.

The conclusion drawn in this section is that the constructions which appear to violate the Generalized Theta Criterion in fact have suspect categorial analyses. It can be plausibly argued that either the complement-taking head, as with DegP, or the complement itself, as with gerunds, is categorially weak, being neutral between two categories.

This interpretation of apparently mixed projections makes it possible to maintain the view that only lexical categories are free to take many different kinds of complements. Functional categories are highly limited. Under Extended Projection each is limited to a very small set of possible complements, given the F-value requirement to be met and the categorial requirement to be met. Apparently mixed projections turn out to be consistent with this claim, once they are viewed as embodying category neutrality.

Finally, I should emphasize that it is only under the theory of Extended Projection that there has to be any interesting categorial relationship between a functional head and its complement in the first place. It is the fact that the complement must form an extended projection with the head, and the fact that to do this it must match the F-head in category, that entails the relationship between the two. In the absence of such principles governing the organization of phrase structure, any arbitrary combination of F-head and complement will be allowed.

1.4.6 Complementizers and Prepositions

According to the theory proposed here, complementizers and prepositions are just members of the verbal and nominal categories respectively, like determiners and tense. The proposal that C stands in the same relationship to IP and VP as P does to DP and NP is similar to that of van Riemsdijk (1978) and Emonds (1985) in treating P and C in a parallel fashion: the difference is that P and C are of different categories in the present proposal, whereas Emonds analyzes them as belonging to the same category (although such comparisons can be a bit misleading because the notion of a "category" is not held constant across the alternatives). I take the fact that the distribution of PP and

CP are similar, which Emonds argues for, not to show that they are of the same category, but to show that they have similar functional status – i.e. they are the most functionally elaborated phrases in their category. Likewise, VP and NP are similar in having a highly restricted distribution, not because they are of the same category, but because they are both without functional elaboration, being projections of lexical heads. Both C and P show significant complexities in behavior which make it less than straightforward to see whether the analysis of CP as an extended projection of V and PP as an extended projection of N is correct. Among these complexities is the fact that complementizers can sometimes take CPs as complements, as prepositions can take PPs. The question is whether by applying notions like "lexical" versus "functional" and "extended projection" we can make sense out of their behavior.

The hypothesis that C, and hence CP, is verbal in category is not obviously correct, but it is important to bear in mind that the external distribution of CPs is certainly not what is expected of a nominal: for example CPs are generally impossible after prepositions (see below), grammatical as complements to passive verbs (*It is believed [that this man robbed a bank in California]*), and occur as relative clauses (*The man [that Mary met] was the robber*).

The fact that complementizers can occur in combinations has been amply demonstrated e.g. Koster 1987, Suñer 1991, Cheng 1991, Bhatt and Yoon 1992, Rizzi 1997, Ackema 2001. One example of this, from Bhatt and Yoon 1992, is given in (36).

(36) Bill-un [John-i   wa-ss-**ta-ko**]   sayngkakhanta.
      Bill-TOP John-NOM come-past-DECL-SUB thinks
      "Bill thinks that John came"

In Bhatt and Yoon's analysis of Korean complementation, the subordinating complementizer *ko* takes as its complement a projection headed by the declarative complementizer *ta*. (The reverse embedding relationship is impossible).

Assuming that the entire complement to the matrix verb is a single extended projection, how can this be accommodated into the theory? The notion that there is just one entity called a "complementizer" is clearly incorrect; instead, we posit that UG admits two or more such heads. Provided that they stand in the appropriate functional relationship, as encoded in their F-values, they will combine into an extended projection. If, for example, the F-value of a subordinating complementizer is 17, and that of a type marking complementizer is 15, the constituent *John-i wa-ss-**ta-ko*** in (36) will be admitted. (Section 1.5 offers a view of cross-linguistic variation in functional heads, along with further evidence from Korean, based on (56) below.)

So in the Korean case, we can identify two distinct complementizer heads and assign them two distinct F-values. This is not always possible, as the following Spanish examples, from M. Suñer p.c., demonstrate.

(37) a. Luis dijo que cuántos libros (que) deben leer los estudiantes para ese curso.
          L said that how many books (that) must read the students for that course

      b. Luis dijo que si que lo podía hacer él.
          L said that yes that it could do he (that he could do it)

Here there are two occurrences of the same complementizer, *que*. Positing two instances of *que* with different F-values seems to miss the point here; a better analysis would maintain the unity of *que* and give it only one F-value. If *que* always has the same F-value, the complements to *dijo* do form a single extended projection under the second version of (4): "The F-value of X is not higher than the F-value of YP." So this version of the theory accommodates multiple occurrences of a single functional head, such as we see in (37).

Independent principles will limit the occurrence of multiples such as these. Where the two identically-headed projections both have empty specifiers, their combination is eliminated by the economy of structure (see Grimshaw 2001, 2003).

(38) *Luis dijo que que deben leer los estudiantes muchos libros para ese curso.
       L said that that must read the students many books for that course

The co-occurrence of syntactically or semantically mutually contradictory heads is ruled out. Korean has another type-marking complementizer for interrogatives. Since it occurs in the same structural position as *ta* (Bhatt and Yoon 1992), it must have the same F-value as *ta*. Therefore the definition of extended projection which allows elements with identical F-values to combine will admit both the interrogative head and the declarative head in a single extended projection, allowing a structure which is of course ill-formed. Surely the theory of Extended Projection does not need to explain why a complement or main clause cannot be simultaneously interrogative and declarative. Rather the theory of sentence types and their semantics already tells us that this is not a possibility.

Provided, then, that we take the definition of extended projection which allows heads and projections of the same F-value to combine, and that we admit the existence of not just one element called a "complementizer" but a class of such elements with potentially different functional contributions and hence different F-values, complementizer combinations are consistent with Extended Projection, setting aside some of the complexities discussed in the references cited.

Prepositions provide a more immediate challenge for Extended Projection. They show evidence of behaving like lexical heads, most clearly in the range of complements that they take, perhaps also in the nature of their meanings. On the other hand, prepositions also show evidence of behaving as functional heads in forming an extended projection with their complement. In addition to pied-piping, further evidence comes from head movement, agreement, and feature projection (Sections 1.4 and 1.5)[25]. These all support the position that P can be a functional category.

Since Jackendoff 1973 it has been widely recognized that Ps can take PP complements – see also Emonds 1985. We see this in examples like (39):

(39) a. Since before the party, he hasn't seen her.
      b. Down toward the children, the hot lava poured.
      c. From inside the house, a loud noise came.

These preposed PPs must be constituents by normal assumptions. Note also that *from* takes an obligatory complement (*A loud noise came from*), supporting the view that *inside the house* is the complement to *from* in (39).

The fact that prepositions take PPs as complements is not by itself particularly problematic for Extended Projection. The theory predicts that Ps can take PP complements if both have the same F-value, or if the value of the c-commanding P is higher than that of the PP. In the latter case, Ps must be able to vary in F-value, as just proposed for complementizers.

It is often suggested, though, that prepositions are, or can be, lexical heads, which take a variety of complements, including prepositional phrases. Most studies of prepositions have concluded that prepositions are not unified with respect to the lexical/functional distinction. Jackendoff's analysis in 1977 includes prepositions which are [+Comp], the feature specification of lexical heads, and some which are [−Comp], the

---

[25]We might also look for evidence from the pronominal system, which contains pro-PPs: *there, then, where, when.* If pro-forms correspond to single functional units, the existence of pro-PPs is evidence that PPs can be functional units, i.e. extended projections.

feature specification of functional heads. Hestvik (1991) distinguishes theta-marking prepositions from those with no theta-marking capacities by their effect on binding domains for anaphors and pronouns, see also Koster (1985). Van Riemdsijk (1990), Zwarts (1995) and Zeller (2001) conclude that some Dutch and German postpositions are functional in character, taking prepositional phrases (with lexical heads) as complements.

Abney (1987: 43–45) suggests that the criteria slightly restated in (40) distinguish lexical from functional heads, recognizing that these properties provide a rule-of-thumb rather than a firmly established and principled set of characteristics. (See also the application of these in Giusti 1997.)

(40)   Functional heads:
- belong to a closed lexical class;
- can be phonologically or morphologically dependent on other material;
- take only one kind of complement;
- have complements which are not arguments (i.e. functional heads are not theta-markers);
- are inseparable from their complement (e.g. they do not occur intransitively and cannot be "stranded");
- lack "descriptive content," making only a second order semantic contribution.

Zwarts (1995) applies criteria of this kind in arguing that the directional prepositions of Dutch fall into two classes, one functional and one lexical. As directionals, *van*, "from," *naar* "to" and *tot* "to" are functional. (The first two have another use which Zwarts analyzes as lexical.) In contrast, the directionals *uit* "out of," *door* "through," *langs* "along," *om* "around," *over* "over, across" and *voorbij* "past" are lexical. The functional prepositions are never intransitive, do not appear in compounds, do not allow extraction of their complement even when it is an R-pronoun (van Riemsdijk 1978); always precede their complement, and do not take PP complements. The lexical prepositions can be intransitive, form compounds, allow R-pronoun complements to extract, can follow their complements and can take DP and PP complements. Zwarts' proposal is that these differences follow from core properties of functional versus lexical heads.

There are several reasons why application of the criteria in (40) is not straightforward. The criteria are maximally helpful only if they coincide, but often they don't. Many of them are difficult to apply – does a preposition like *behind* have descriptive content?; does it theta-mark its complement when it is the head of an adjunct?; when it is the head of an argument? Is it a member of a comparatively small open class, or of a closed class? Sometimes, other work partially contradicts one of the assumptions, as is the case with the conclusion of Lobeck (1990) regarding the ellipsis of complements to functional heads. Finally, in investigating heads, such as prepositions, we find many, many differences among them. Some may be pre- and some post-positional, some locative, some temporal, some apparently meaningful and some meaningless (such as *of*). Only one of these important differences can truly correspond to the lexical/functional distinction (if the theory is correct, that is) – so which one is it? Prepositions seem to be a very heterogeneous group, all are heads which are not Vs and which generally take a DP complement, but with not much else in common. The "lexical" versus "functional" distinction is just not rich enough to characterize the varying behavior of prepositions.

If it is correct that some prepositions are lexical, is this consistent with Extended Projection? The answer is that it is, in principle. It simply means that some prepositions have the F-value of lexical heads, and some have higher F-values. A proposal along these lines for nouns has been made by Vos 1999 and van Riemsdijk 1998. Of course such proposals raise the issue of the exact content of the label "preposition" or "noun," but this issue arises anyway, and is not particular to Extended Projection.

Is this the right solution for the prepositions in (39) with PP complements? It predicts, following the reasoning in Section 1.4.3, that there will be no pied-piping of the higher preposition, so the pied-piping structures which should be grammatical are those in (41):[26]

(41)　a.　*Before which party has he not seen her since?

　　　b.　Toward which children did the hot lava pour down?

　　　c.　*Inside which house did a loud noise come from?

These are all strongly ungrammatical, apart from b., which is possible because *poured down toward the children* has two analyses, as Jackendoff (1973) shows. In one of these analyses *down* and *toward* are independent constituents, so *toward the children* is not a complement of *down*.

When the entire complex PP is fronted, which should be completely impossible if the higher preposition is lexical, the result is the examples in (42). These are distinctly awkward, but far better than the previous alternatives.

---

[26] For discussion of the extraction of PPs from PPs see van Riemsdijk 1978, Koster 1987, Cinque 1990.

(42)   a.   ?Since before which party has he not seen her?

     b.   ?Down toward which children did the hot lava pour?

     c.   ?From inside which house did a loud noise come?

Moreover, if these prepositions have the same status when they take DP complements, i.e. if they are lexical, we are left with no explanation for pied-piping of the preposition in cases like (43):

(43)   a.   Since which party has he not seen her?

     b.   Down which street did the hot lava pour?

     c.   From which house did a loud noise come?

In contrast, if the first preposition is functional, the pied-piping facts are partly explained[27].

The conclusion is, then, that prepositions may have a range of F-values. Setting aside the possibility that they may be lexical heads, we arrive at an analysis along the lines of (44):

(44)   *since* $F4$ or $F3$
      before $F3$
      the $F1$
      party $F0$

These F-values are of course illustrative only. Since all of these heads are nominal, they can form an extended projection with *since* as the highest head, then *before*, then *the*, and finally the lexical head noun, giving *since before the party*. The analysis also predicts that *since* can combine directly with *the party*; the F-value of *since* is higher than that of the DP and they match in category. So we do not need to posit two different cases of *since*, or two F-values for it. If *since* is assigned $F4$, Extended Projection will not allow it to head the complement to *before*, ruling out **before since the party*. If there is an independent explanation for the ungrammaticality of this combination, the F-value of *since* can be identical to that of *before*, under the definition of extended projection which allows a functional head to have the same F-value as its complement.

This does not complete the analysis of prepositions in terms of Extended Projection, however, because a preposition can take a *clausal* complement (i.e. a verbal extended projection in the present terms) under certain circumstances. Many adjunct clauses in English are introduced by a element which certainly looks like a preposition with a

---

[27]Only partly, because we do not know why the examples involving stranding are ungrammatical. If the wh feature obligatorily projects to the highest PP node, why is preposition stranding ever possible? See note 17.

bare IP complement (see Dubinsky and Williams 1995).[28]

(45) a. He hasn't seen her since the party started.

   b. We left after they arrived.

Other languages tolerate prepositions in combination with propositional complements, as illustrated by the following Spanish examples (Suñer p.c.):[29]

(46) a. Luis se escapó sin que lo vieran los guardias
      L escaped without that the guards see (subjunctive) him

   b. Luis cerró la puerta para que no lo interrumperan más
      L closed the door for that (they) didn't interrupt him any
      more

Evidently prepositions admit complements from the verbal category. Assuming that these prepositions are not lexical heads, they can take complements only if they match their complement in category. This is possible only if the prepositions are verbal or the complement is nominal. Since I find it hard to envisage a successful analysis of structures like *the party started* as nominal, I pursue the first of these two alternatives: prepositions have some properties in common with verbal heads.

As a first step, we hypothesize that some "prepositions" are complementizers as well: they have two syntactic categories. (The powerful affinity between complementizers and prepositions has been emphasized in a number of studies. See Emonds 1985, Cinque 1990 on *a, di* as Ps and Cs in Italian; and Kayne 1997, 1998, 1999.[30]) Heads like *that*, *while*, and *although* are only verbal and take only verbal complements,

---

[28] A handful of introductory clause elements, perhaps those which are not themselves heads, co-occur with *that* (*now that, so that, . . .*), but in general no *that* is possible: *. . . since that the party started.* *. . . before that you arrived.*

[29] Cinque (1990: 35–36) argues that Italian does not usually admit sentential complements within subcategorized PPs, while they are possible in adjuncts.

[30] The most extreme position that we might take is that there is no difference between "P" and "C." "P" is a convenient name for an X which takes a DP complement, "C" is what we call an X which takes an IP complement, but there is no real difference in category between them, any more than there is between a verb which takes a DP and a verb which takes a CP. This is more or less the position proposed in Emonds 1985. He establishes an intriguing number of parallels between "CPs" and "PPs." This proposal is not quite consistent with Extended Projection. If P and C belong to one syntactic category, this category can match nominal complements, forming extended projections with them, or it can match verbal complements, forming extended projections with them, but not both. This motivates my decision to pursue category neutrality for some prepositions, rather than category identity for prepositions and complementizers. A further difference is that category identity requires appeal to subcategorization or selection to distinguish between Ps/Cs which take DP complements and those which take IP complements, and this is inconsistent with type-category selection as laid out in Section 1.6.

i.e. clauses. Heads like *during, despite*, and the locatives and direction-als are only nominal and take only nominal complements[31]. The last group of heads is both verbal and nominal, and takes both clausal and nominal complements. The following data illustrate these properties:

(47) a. Only verbal (C): *that, while, although*

      b. Only nominal (P): *during, despite*, locatives, directionals

      c. Both verbal and nominal (P and C): *after, before, since, until, for, to, from,*[32] *than, as*

(48) a. They announced *that* the event would begin at 6.

      b. They announced the event.

      c. *They announced *that* the event.

(49) a. He saw her *while* the event was taking place.

      b. He saw her *during/*while* the event.

      c. *He saw her *during* the event was taking place.

(50) a. He saw her *after* the event took place.

      b. He saw her *after* the event.

      c. They were anxious *for* good weather.

      d. They were anxious *for* the weather to be good.

How can a head be both verbal and nominal, without having two separate lexical entries, and thus forfeiting its fundamental unity? We can extend the logic of category neutrality from Section 1.4.5, positing that the prepositions which take both nominal and verbal complements are neutral between nominal and verbal, just as degree heads are neu-tral between adverbs and adjectives. These prepositions will then be able to combine with DPs or with other PPs to form single extended projections; they will also be able to combine with IPs or CPs and again form extended projections. Thus (47) should be revised to state that the final group of prepositions is *neither nominal nor verbal*, rather than that they are *both nominal and verbal*:

(51) a. *that, while, although*   [−Nom]

      b. *during, despite*, locatives, directionals   [+Nom]

      c. *after, before, since, until, for, to, from, than, as* [+/−Nom]

---

[31]On the minimal contrast between *while* and *during*, and *although* and *despite* (see Larson 1990: 175).

[32]*from* occurs as a complementizer-like element with gerundives: *I prevented them from completing their work.* See Rosenbaum 1967, Postal 1974, Baltin 1995, Landau 2002.

This solution fully accommodates clausal complements to prepositions, even the fact that the prepositions *can combine with each other*:

(52)   a.   He hasn't seen her since before the party started.

   b.   We stayed until after they arrived.

In order to combine with the IP *the party started* with DPs like *the party*, the preposition *before* must be neutral between nominal and verbal. By the logic of percolation of the category of a complement, the entire phrase *before the party started* is verbal in category. In order to combine with this larger verbal constitutent, and with DPs like *the party*, the preposition *since* must similarly be neutral between nominal and verbal. Again the entire phrase headed by *since* is verbal in this case. Provided that the F-value of *since* is either the same as, or higher than, the F-value of *before*, as already established, the entire adjunct is a single extended projection.

(53)

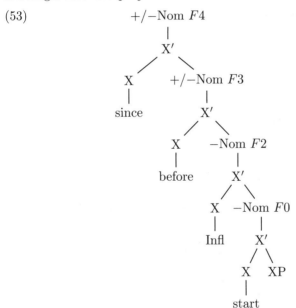

There is another possible way to develop the key idea here, and it uses a version of the line pursued in van Riemsdijk 1990, 1998. He adopts a feature system in which N is $+N/-V$, V is $+V/-N$, and P is $-V/-N$ (Chomsky 1970a, Muysken 1983). This makes prepositions unique in being negatively specified for both categorial features. Now, suppose that we relax the category matching requirement on extended projections. Instead of requiring that the categorial features match, the definition can allow categorial features to switch in one direction but not the other, so that a −F head can take a +F complement and form an extended projection, but a +F head can never take a −F complement in a single projection. This is not what van Riemsdijk himself proposes. His definitions require full categorial identity within a projection, so a preposition can only form a projection with a PP complement. However, he proposes a principle which rules out positive specifications of a feature over negative specifications for the feature. This is part of his set of conditions which govern all complement taking relations (not just those that govern (extended) projections), so my suggestion in the previous paragraph puts his principle to a different use.

Under this solution, PPs can form extended projections with any complement, since prepositions are negatively specified for all categories. It is still necessary to distinguish between prepositions which take clausal complements and those which take only nominals. Subcategorization or case features will still be required so that individual prepositions can determine the category of their complement. However, this analysis would be hard to reconcile with the theory of Type-Category selection (Section 1.6), so I conclude that the solution based on category neutrality is preferable.

1.5   Functional Heads and Universal Grammar

Lying behind the structural hypotheses adopted in research on functional projections is an underlying assumption about how phrases are constructed, which Extended Projection illuminates. The assumption is that functional heads supply information which serves to integrate the phrase into a larger syntactic and semantic domain. Just as a well-formed word must have all of the morphemes required by the grammar of the language, so a well-formed phrase must be functionally complete – it must be specified in every required way. The question is, of course, what counts as functionally complete, and does this vary from language to language?

At one extreme is the position adopted recently and most stringently by Cinque, that every projection is present, even if it contains no overt head, in the structure of every sentence of every language: see, for example, the concluding discussion of his study of adverbs (Cinque 1999: 141). The problem with such theories is that they side-step the problem of explaining what is overtly present in any given sentence; without principles governing overt and covert realization, we are shifting a large part of the burden of explanation into some unknown domain.[33] It is, however, extremely attractive to develop the hypothesis that functional heads are not organized radically differently in different languages, and Cinque's results certainly support this view. So here I will sketch an alternative position which allows for some inter- and intra-linguistic variation but is still highly constrained.

Following Zwarts 1992, Chomsky 1995, and Cinque 1999, I assume that universal grammar provides a set of possible functional specifications. The verbal set includes subordinator, type, mood, tense and so forth; the nominal set includes locative, definiteness, quantification and whatever the other possible heads prove to be. These are universally organized in a hierarchy. While under Cinque's hypothesis this hierarchy is realized in a universal tree structure, in terms of Extended Projection it is realized in a fixed hierarchy of F-value. Suppose, then, that there are 40 verbal functional specifications allowed by UG. A head encoding the highest specification will have $F40$ in its lexical entry, and the lowest will have $F1$, and lexical heads will have $F0$. Now suppose that languages can choose whether or not to include each functional specification as a head in their lexical inventory. Language A may therefore have heads $\{F40, F28, F16, F2\}$, while Language B has $\{F33, F25, F14, F13, F12, F3\}$, and so forth. This is illustrated by the chart in (54).

---

[33]Cinque proposes that lexically unrealized heads are associated with an unmarked interpretation for the functional information carried by heads of their type.

(54)

Functional Heads Defined by UG	Functional Heads Included in the Grammar of Language A	Functional Heads Included in the Grammar of Language B
$F1$		
$F2$	$\checkmark$	
$F3$		$\checkmark$
...		
$F12$		$\checkmark$
$F13$		$\checkmark$
$F14$		$\checkmark$
$F15$		
$F16$	$\checkmark$	
...		
$F25$		$\checkmark$
$F28$	$\checkmark$	
$F33$		$\checkmark$
$F40$	$\checkmark$	
...		

The principles of Extended Projection will impose a hierarchical structure on these heads. Since a head with a given F-value cannot take a head with a higher F-value as its complement, $F40$ will c-command $F28$ if both are present in the structure, similarly $F26$ will c-command $F15$, and so forth. So the position in the hierarchy of F-heads will be fixed in the theory, although the *absolute* position in the structure of a phrase can vary from language to language, and from sentence to sentence within a language, depending on the nature of the grammatical constraints that are relevant.[34] Thus structures like (55), where F-values are shown for the boxed nodes only, will be admitted in Language A, but not structures where $F16$ c-commands $F28$, and so forth.

---

[34]If the notion of a "layer" (see especially Rizzi 1997) has real theoretical status, rather than being just a convenient descriptive term, the system of F-values could be elaborated to reflect it, e.g. by associating the heads of each layer with a particular range of F-values, and allowing principles of the theory to refer to these ranges.

(55)

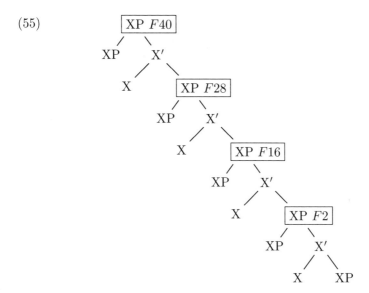

It is not required that every language have the same heads, but it is required that the heads that a language does have follow the principles of Extended Projection.

This hypothesis is consistent with a non-rigid view of syntactic structure: for example, it is consistent with the hypothesis that heads that never occur overtly in the language are not projected in its structures or that heads and projections are present in the structure of a sentence only when they are overt or motivated by some grammatical principle. See Grimshaw 2001, 2003 and references cited there.

There is some cross-linguistic variation in the grammar of functional heads; see for example Cinque 1999 on the special properties of agreement and negation, and also Laka 1990, Ouhalla 1990. Following Cinque's strategy, we should not necessarily conclude from this that the universalist theory is to be abandoned. Cinque's proposal is that negation and agreement show surface variation because they can each appear in more than one position in the hierarchy of functional heads (see especially Zanuttini 1997 on negation). Languages may then differ in which of the positions they realize. I will assume, in line with this view, that the relative position of functional heads is entirely universal, with surface differences depending on which of the universally available functional heads occur in the language. Of course other factors, such as head movement, may also affect the surface appearance of functional head combinations.

Despite the fixed relative position of functional heads, several studies suggest that functional information can be encoded in more than one position; a grammatical property or feature can be associated with one node in one language and another node in a second language, or that it can be associated in various ways within a single language. From the perspective of Extended Projection, this finding is not unexpected. If we view functional heads (and some bound morphemes) as contributing functional information, and if this information projects through the extended projection, then the exact location of the information really does not matter in the end. Provided that a feature is on a head of the extended projection, its value will project to the entire extended projection, no matter which head it originates from.

Combining the fixed hierarchy of functional information imposed by F-values with the principles of Extended Projection, we predict that alternative positioning of functional information will always adhere to the hierarchy, and will be strictly limited to the choice among alternative positions within an extended projection. This corresponds approximately to Haider's notion (Haider 1988) of "indirect representation" of a functional head.

Variation in the complementizer system has been established, involving type and subordination (Bhatt and Yoon 1992). They argue that the English complementizer *that* encodes both a type (declarative) and subordinate status in a single morpheme, whereas Korean and Kashmiri preserve separate morphemes for each component, as discussed in Section 1.4.6. English *that* introduces clauses that are both subordinate and declarative, whereas Korean *ko* introduces all subordinate clauses, and Korean *ta* introduces all declaratives.

(56) a. John-i   wa-ss-**ta**.
          John-NOM come-PAST-DECL
          "John came"

      b. Bill-un [John-i   wa-ss-**ta-ko**]   sayngkakhanta.
          Bill-TOP John-NOM come-past-DECL-SUB thinks
          "Bill thinks that John came"

      c. Bill-un [John-i   wa-ss-**nya-ko**]   mwulessta.
          Bill-TOP John-NOM come-past-INTER-SUB asked
          "Bill asked if John came"

English thus "conflates" two kinds of functional information into a single head. This can be represented by assigning one head multiple F-values, as illustrated in (57) using arbitrary illustrative F-values. Applying the definition of an extended projection in the obvious way predicts that the English complementizer must be above all other clausal heads and that the subordinating element c-commands the type element in Korean.

(57) Korean: *ko* $[+V\ -N]$ $\{F6\}$
            ta $[+V\ -N]$ $\{F5\}$
      English: *that* $[+V\ -N]$ $\{F5, F6\}$

Irish has a series of introductory clause particles differentiated into "nonpast" and "past" forms (Chung and McCloskey 1987), as illustrated in the contrasting pair in (58) and (59):

(58) an fear a   labhrann   tú leis
      the man Comp speak (Pres) you with-him
      "the man that you speak to"

(59) an fear ar   labhair   tú leis
      the man Comp speak (Past) you with-him

Chung and McCloskey suggest that the particle is a syntactically complex form constructed from C and I, although there is some morphological complexity and suppletion involved, as in the case of P + D combinations discussed below. (See Hendrick 2000 for a recent discussion of complementizers in Celtic.) In the present terms, these forms can be analyzed as in (60), in parallel with the previously discussed cases:

(60) Irish:
        a   [verbal] $\{F5, F6\}$ non-past
        ar   [verbal] $\{F5, F6\}$ past
        labhrann   [verbal] $\{F0, F5\}$ non-past
        labhair   [verbal] $\{F0, F5\}$ past

In these cases, tense appears twice in the extended projection, both on V and on a head conflating tense and the complementizer. The presence of the tense on the verb is not required for well-formedness of the extended projection. It is presumably forced by the morphology: a verb stem with no inflection would violate morphological well-formedness. Recall that functional information can be encoded more than once in a given extended projection, subject to consistency (see the discussion of Korean in Section 1.4.2 for an extreme case).

Irish also has negative complementizers in Chung and McCloskey's analysis, as does Basque in the analysis of Laka 1990. She argues that Basque NegP (which is head initial, unlike other functional projections in Basque) c-commands tense, while the opposite c-command relations hold in English. Flexibility of the positioning of negation has been demonstrated in many studies: Zanuttini 1997, Cinque 1999, Ouhalla 1997.

Analyses of "verb second" systems have exploited the idea that a functional feature can be realized on different functional head positions in different languages. Holmberg and Platzack (1995) argue that there is a parametric choice with respect to a finiteness feature, which can be in C (for V2 languages) or in I (for non-V2 languages). This feature attracts the V, hence explaining V2 effects. (They also suggest that C carries a feature for number in Icelandic, but not in German.) Rizzi (1990) suggests that Tense must occur on the highest head position in the clause marked as +I. This is the head of IP in non-V2 languages and the head of CP in V2 systems. The shared idea is that the V2 languages can mark C with something that the non-V2 languages mark I for. More recently, Pesetsky and Torrego (2001) argue that an uninterpretable Tense feature on C forces T-to-C movement. They speculate (n. 77 p. 418) that the presence of this feature on C might be related to the status of CP as an extended projection of T and V. In their proposal, nominative case is the same uninterpretable feature on D^{35}. These various proposals can be modeled following the general lines of the analyses given above: all of them presuppose the naturalness of the idea that properties might be distributed within an extended projection in different ways in different languages or different structures.

When its complement is null, the Irish P inflects morphologically in response to the number and person of its (missing) object. The forms (1st singular, 2nd singular, 3rd masculine singular etc.) of *le* are given in (61) from McCloskey and Hale (1984: 506–507):

(61) a. le "with"
S1 liom, S2 leat, MS3 leis, FS3 léithi
P1 linn, P2 libh, P3 leofa

    b. Bhí mé ag caint leofa inné.
was I talk(PROG) with (P3) yesterday
"I was talking to them yesterday"

    c. *leofa iad / siad
"with (P3) them / they"

From this we conclude that functional features which are normally encoded on pronouns (which I assume are cases of D), can be encoded on P instead. This possibility seems to be instantiated also in the suppletive prepositional forms found in Romance and Germanic languages,

---

[35]The privileged relationship of subjects as the specifier of the verbal extended projection (see the discussion of Korean plurals in Section 1.4.2) may address the concern they raise on this matter, and provide a rationale for this distribution of the T feature. See their n. 77.

such as the French examples in (62), where the preposition *à* "to" does not occur with the plural definite article, a single form replacing both. Similarly in German (see (63) from Beerman 1990) a suppletive form occurs in place of both the P and the D.

(62) J'ai donné un cadeau **aux** enfants.
      I have given a present to the children

(63) Johann geht **ins** Haus.
      Johann goes in-neut/sing/acc house

Here, the forms *aux* and *ins* are complex in the sense that they appear in contexts where separate P and D are normally found, and encode the information otherwise encoded in D and P. Following the analysis of complementizers above, these complex forms can be analyzed as having multiple *F*-values:

(64) French:
      $à$ [nominal] $\{F6\}$
      les   [nominal] $\{F5\}$
      aux   [nominal] $\{F5, F6\}$

A point of interest here is that Extended Projection does not itself predict the complementarity between the complex form *aux* and one of the simplex heads, P and D. In particular, a head which is $F6$ taking a complement which is $\{F5, F6\}$ is consistent with the most natural extension of the definition of an extended projection to heads with multiple *F*-values, which will require that no *F*-value of a complement can be higher than any *F*-value of the complement-taking head within a single extended projection. A head which is F6 cannot, by this definition, take a complement headed by an item which is $\{F7, F6\}$.

This definition allows a head which is $\{F5, F6\}$ to take a complement which is $F5$ to form an extended projection. This may be a flaw in the proposal. On the other hand, the complementarity of these heads would follow from Economy of Structure, in the model of Grimshaw 2001 and 2003. The additional projection headed by a D or a P does not contribute any additional functional information, since what its head encodes is already present by virtue of the presence of the complex head. The presence of the additional projection is necessarily costly (it violates at least one of a set of constraints on well-formed projections (see Grimshaw 2001, 2003 for the details)). Hence the structure without the higher preposition is optimal and the only grammatical possibility.

In sum, we posit a universal inventory of functional specifications, with languages differing as to which of them they realize and which of them they realize as a single morpheme, but not in their relative

position in hierarchical structure. The fact that relative positions are
fixed is due to the requirements of Extended Projection. Some properties, such as tense or number, may be realized on more than one
functional head; due to the effects of projection the information they
represent will be recorded as properties of the entire extended projection. Head movement can be responsible for further alteration of the
core functional hierarchy. The fundamental claim of this paper is that
the domain over which the hierarchy is defined is that of an extended
projection, not just a collection of phrases linked together by selection.

1.6 Selection and Projection

Extended Projection holds that the relationship between a functional
head and its complement is one of *projection*. In contrast the relationship between a lexical head and its complement is one of *selection*. In
Abney 1987 and following work on the theory of functional heads *selection* is posited as the basic mechanism regulating the organization
of phrase structure. C is said to select IP, I to select VP, D to select
NP, and so forth. Thus the fact that some combinations are possible,
and that others, such as C with an NP complement, never occur, is
attributed to lexical selectional properties of individual heads: selection is the fundamental principle controlling the internal structure of
syntactic expressions.

The theory of Extended Projection offers an alternative. In this theory there is another mechanism at work inside an extended projection –
projection itself. The fact that C takes an IP complement and I a VP
complement, for example, depends on syntactic category and F-values
which permit them to form an extended projection. Moreover, because
of the Generalized Theta Criterion, they *must* form an extended projection since neither C nor I is a lexical head. It follows that C can take
only IP or another verbal projection with an appropriate F-value. And
of course the same reasoning holds for systems which include Agr, T,
Asp and so forth. Functional heads will combine only with complements
that they form extended projections with.

What lexical heads occur with is not determined at all by projection, since there is no relationship of (extended) projection between
a lexical head and its complement. Thus the theory of selection must
take responsibility for regulating lexical heads and their complements.
So functional heads take complements that they form extended projections with, and lexical heads take complements that they select.

The constraints imposed on F-heads and their complements are *more
restrictive* if the relationship is one of projection than if selection is

involved; in fact I believe that there is nothing *substantive* to the claim that the relationship between an F-head and its complement is one of selection. All that is claimed is that there is a relationship (and perhaps that the relationship is local, although see the discussion of locality in Section 1.4), and that the relationship is such that the head can lexically stipulate what its complement can be. Calling the relationship "selection" does not bring to bear a set of principled restrictions; it merely allows the description of any observed combination.

For example, what rules out a grammar in which Tense selects CP and the complementizer selects VP? In such a language a subordinator would occur below Tense. This is presumably not a possible linguistic system, but the selectional statements involved are impeccable. To consider another example, suppose A selects a BP as its complement, and B selects a CP as its complement. Nothing prevents C from selecting AP, perhaps among other options. This yields a language in which the same head occurs both above and below some other head, again presumably not possible, but easily described using selection.

Via Extended Projection, F-heads and their complements are regulated through a hypothesis about categories and the universal hierarchy of functional heads (Section 1.5), which connects them to other aspects of the theory, not through isolated stipulations about what goes with what. To say that the relationship is one of (extended) projection is to say that its properties follow from the same theory that constrains projection in the first place: the definition of extended head/projection and the theory of categories and functional values according to which the content of an F-head determines where it falls on the hierarchy (modulo the comments on negation and agreement above). The positions of Tense, subordinator, and type marker on the universal hierarchy make tense with a CP complement impossible. If an F-head A can take a BP as its complement and the F-head of BP can take a CP as its complement, it is impossible for the head of C to take AP as its complement, unless all three F-heads have the same *F*-value. In this way, properties of the relationship between F-heads and their complements follow from a more general theory of projection. If selection is responsible for these relationships, the relationships are virtually unconstrained and disconnected from other aspects of the theory.

Of course the theory of selection could be supplemented with the requirement that heads can only select for elements lower on the hierarchy. But this supplementary principle would have to be limited to functional heads – it certainly doesn't hold of lexical heads. This is my point: the properties of selection and those of F-head/complement combinations are just not the same, and giving them the same name, "selection," does not solve this problem.

Extended Projection explains apparent instances of selection by F-heads, as in *for someone to do something* versus *that someone did something*, as we have already seen (in Section 1.4). The relationship between *for* and *to*, and between *that* and a non-infinitival inflection, is simply one of agreement through the extended projection.

Projection explains the limited range of complements for F-heads. The complement to an F-head is subject to category and *F*-value requirements, neither of which constrains complements to L-heads, which can therefore take complements of all syntactic categories (up to the effects of other principles such as case theory).

Pollock (1989), Zanuttini (1996, 1997), Laka (1990), Haegeman (1995), Potsdam (1997) and others argue that certain negative elements head functional projections which participate in clause structure (in the present terms they form part of the verbal extended projection). Zanuttini, for example, shows that Italian *non* appears preverbally, preceding auxiliary verbs, and occurs only in clauses containing a tense (Zanuttini 1996) or an expression of mood (Zanuttini 1997). This is why *non* on an imperative, which she argues is a defective form, is ungrammatical, as in (65). For a negative imperative, the imperative verb is replaced by a different form, which does meet the requirements of the negative head, as in (66); these examples are from Zanuttini 1997: 108.

(65)   *Non telefona!   (true imperative)
       neg call
       "Don't call!"   (2nd sg)

(66)   Non telefonarle! (suppletive imperative)
       neg to-call her (infinitival form)
       "Don't call her!" (2nd sg)

These facts, plus the core observation that negation precedes tense in Italian, motivate the hypothesis that the structure of negative clauses is the one given in (67), where Neg takes a MoodP complement.

(67)

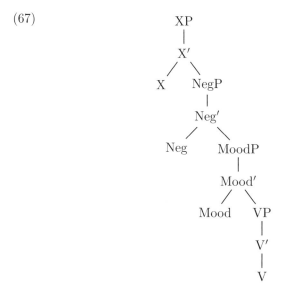

Zanuttini suggests that Italian Neg is a head which always selects MoodP, hence it never occurs with defective verbs. (Laka's (1990) account of Basque negation posits a special relationship between Neg and T, although it is expressed in terms of the "Tense C-command Condition," rather than through selection.) So in (67), X selects NegP and Neg selects MoodP. Now if selection is responsible for the structure in this case, what happens when Neg and NegP are absent, as in (68)?[36]

(68)

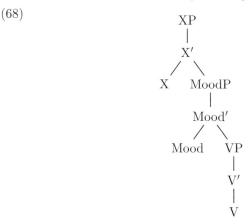

Here X is occurring with a MoodP complement, and not a NegP complement. A mechanical solution could say that X must select both

---

[36]Needless to say this problem does not arise if we adopt the position that NegP is always present. See Section 1.5 for some discussion of this possibility.

NegP and MoodP, but this does not shed much light on the issue. There is no other head which obligatorily "selects" NegP, or which "anti-selects" Neg; but why not? It looks as if the higher head X is not sensitive to the presence or absence of the NegP; it simply makes no difference to the relationship between X and MoodP whether the NegP is present or not. The head which is on top of NegP occurs with NegP or MoodP indiscriminately, apparently unable to distinguish NegP from MoodP. But there is no principled account for this under the selection theory. We cannot even say that NegP is somehow ignored by selection, because selection is supposed to be responsible for the position of NegP in a clause.

The simplest solution to the problem of such intervening optional heads rests on projection. Whatever F-value X has is either higher than that of Mood or the same. So MoodP and XP will form an extended projection, and whatever the features or properties of the Mood head are, they will project to XP. If Neg happens to intervene in the structure, its F-value places it between X and Mood, but the relationship between X and Mood is otherwise unchanged. Properties of Mood still project to XP, and hence properties of Mood and properties of X must be consistent. This is why NegP can intervene between XP and MoodP without fundamentally changing their relationship.

To complete the picture, we must explain why *non* cannot occur with some non-finite complements such as imperatives and participles, as Zanuttini argues. If these verb forms carry the feature [−mood], this feature will project up through the entire extended projection, in accordance with the principles discussed in Section 1.4. (Of course the feature "mood" is merely illustrative – see Zanuttini's research on the nature of the critical property.) If *non* itself carries the feature [+mood], its feature value will conflict with that of a [−mood] verbal form, and it will only be able to constitute a well-formed extended projection in combination with a mood-marked verbal complement. Thus projection (and more precisely agreement through the projection) determines what Neg can combine with. Selection plays no role.

The same point can be made for any of the functional heads which is omissible. Consider Cinque's hierarchy. The hierarchy of 28 clausal functional heads in (69) is a simplified version of the one given in Cinque 1999: 106.

(69) $\text{Mood}_{\text{Speech act}} > \text{Mood}_{\text{evaluative}} > \text{Mood}_{\text{evidential}} > \text{Mod}_{\text{epistemic}}$
$> \text{T (Past)} > \text{T (Future)} > \text{Mood}_{\text{irrealis}} > \text{Mod}_{\text{necessity}} >$
$\text{Mod}_{\text{possibility}} > \text{Asp}_{\text{habitual}} > \text{Asp}_{\text{repetitive}} > \text{Asp}_{\text{frequentative}} >$
$\text{Mod}_{\text{volitional}} > \text{Asp}_{\text{celerative}} > \text{T (Anterior)} > \text{Asp}_{\text{terminative}} >$
$\text{Asp}_{\text{continuative}} > \text{Asp}_{\text{perfect}} > \text{Asp}_{\text{retrospective}} > \text{Asp}_{\text{proximative}} >$
$\text{Asp}_{\text{durative}} > \text{Asp}_{\text{generic/progressive}} > \text{Asp}_{\text{prospective}} >$
$\text{Asp}_{\text{SgCompletive(I)}} > \text{Asp}_{\text{PlCompletive}} > \text{Voice} > \text{Asp}_{\text{celerative}} >$
$\text{Asp}_{\text{SgCompletive(II)}}$

Suppose that $\text{Asp}_{\text{retrospective}}$ is a head which is present only in some structures in a given language. This means that the head immediately higher in the hierarchy must select for either $\text{Asp}_{\text{retrospective}}$ or $\text{Asp}_{\text{proximative}}$, the next lower head in the hierarchy. Now suppose that $\text{Asp}_{\text{proximative}}$ is in turn omissible. Now the higher head must add $\text{Asp}_{\text{durative}}$ to its list of selected complements, and in addition, $\text{Asp}_{\text{retrospective}}$ must be said to select for either $\text{Asp}_{\text{proximative}}$ or $\text{Asp}_{\text{durative}}$, and so forth. If selection governs well-formedness of head-complement combinations, optionality of heads can be accommodated only by multiplying out the selectional possibilities, and the non-random character of the result cannot be explained.

In contrast, the model in which each of these heads has an F-value determined by its position on the universal hierarchy offers a principled solution to the status of optional heads. Suppose that $\text{Mood}_{\text{Speechact}}$ is $F28$, and $\text{Asp}_{\text{SgCompletive(II)}}$ is $F1$, with the intermediate heads assigned F-values in the obvious way. In a clause which contains all the verbal functional heads of (69), the hierarchical relationships must respect the hierarchy encoded in the F-values. But the same is true of a structure which contains only four of the heads of (69). As pointed out in Section 1.5, Extended Projection will entail that an $F18$ head c-command an $F12$ head, which must c-command an $F6$ head, which must c-command an $F2$ head, when all are present. This is determined by projection, and has nothing to do with selection. So the structural organization of combinations of functional heads follows, regardless of whether every potential functional head occurs in the structure or not.[37]

---

[37]In earlier presentations of this work, I proposed to exclude structures like C-VP by requiring that F-values can differ by at most 1, so that C-VP would not be a well-formed extended projection if VP has a value of 0, and C has an F-value higher than 1. Heads which can intervene between two other heads, without disrupting the extended projection, must have intermediate F-values. For instance, suppose that Neg has an F-value of 1.5, T has a F-value of 1 and C an F-value of 2. Now CP-NegP-TP-VP is a well-formed extended projection, and so is CP-TP-VP. Neg can be omitted without bad consequences, because CP-TP-VP is well-formed. However, T cannot be omitted, because CP-NegP-VP and CP-VP are not well-formed, hence

The last, but not the least, point in support of projection rather than selection as the force behind the organization of functional heads is the theory of selection itself. Because the complement-taking properties of functional heads are not like those of lexical heads, it is hard to construct a constrained theory of selection which encompasses both. In contrast, the theory can be substantially tightened and developed if selection regulates only the relationship between lexical heads and their complements. The particular theory which I propose here is "Type-Category Selection."

Four principles are fundamental to Type-Category Selection. First, only L-heads select, as just discussed. Second, syntactic selection must be distinguished from semantic selection (Grimshaw 1979, Pesetsky 1982). Third, syntactic selection is for syntactic category. Fourth, semantic selection is for semantic type.[38]

Since semantic selection is sensitive to the semantic type of a complement, such as proposition, interrogative, event, action and so forth, it will be able to distinguish among complements of different types. Some F-heads are type-changing; the type of their projection is different from the type of their complement. For example, many researchers have proposed that NP and DP are of different semantic types (Longobardi 1994, Zamparelli 2000), making D a type-changing head. Semantic selection is of course sensitive to the presence or absence of an F-head when its projection belongs to a different semantic type than its complement. However, when an F-head is not type-changing, semantic selection will be oblivious to its presence or absence[39]. Furthermore, since semantic selection is sensitive to semantic type only, it will be unable to detect the syntactic category of a complement, and hence cannot determine the syntactic realization of the complement of a selecting head.

The other important point about Type-Category Selection is that syntactic selection is limited to syntactic category, just as semantic selection is limited to semantic type. The significance of this becomes apparent when we recall that, in the hypothesis developed here, F-value is not a matter of syntactic category, so that CP, IP and VP are all of the same category, as are DP, NP and some PPs. It follows then

---

T cannot be omitted from CPs, and Neg cannot take non-finite verb projections as complements because their F-value is too low. A theory along these lines will connect with some of the issues raised in Section 1.5.

[38]On semantic selection, see Grimshaw 1993, reprinted here as Chapter 2.

[39]What actually counts as a type for selection is an empirical question. There are significant semantic properties, such as definiteness, which are not visible to selection, presumably because they are not type-changing.

that *no head*, whether functional or lexical, *can select the F-value of its complement*.

Selection for interrogatives will clarify how selection works under these assumptions. Consider first the examples in (70).

(70) a. *We wondered whether it was late.

  b. We asked the doorman what the time was.

The verbs *ask* and *wonder* semantically select Q, the type of interrogatives. Both syntactically select the category verbal. Both of these selectional needs are satisfied in (70). However, the two predicates differ in that *ask* also selects for nominal complements, whereas *wonder* does not. As a result we have the contrast in (71), where *wonder* is ungrammatical with a "concealed" question.

(71) a. *We wondered the time.

  b. We asked the doorman the time.

So the contrasts in selection reported in Grimshaw (1979) can be captured in the present theory of selection[40]. Conspicuously, the selection here is between complements of two different categories: nominal and verbal. We see the effects of syntactic selection when we hold the semantic type constant, as in the case just analyzed.

Syntactic selection cannot distinguish among members of a set with the same syntactic category. If a lexical head c-selects for the verbal set it must in principle accept CP, IP and VP as complements. If it c-selects for the nominal set it will accept in principle PP, DP and NP as complements. Since there is no category difference between the members of each set, which members of the category set actually occur with any given head will depend on the effects of other principles of grammar, and also on the effects of semantic selection, but not on syntactic selection.

Therefore selection within a category set is semantic-selection, which is sensitive to semantic type only, and can distinguish members of a category set from one another only when they are of different semantic types. Thus selection by a V for a VP, IP, or CP complement must be semantic selection, for types such as action, event, proposition, as in Rochette 1988, 1990. (If, for example, an "exceptional case-marking" verb selects IP versus CP, the selection must be semantic.) The fact that a verb which selects an action takes a VP, one which selects an event takes an IP, and one which selects a proposition takes a CP is not a matter of syntactic selection. It simply reflects the fact that these are

---

[40]I have not attempted to address optional versus obligatory complements here, so the cases of null complements analyzed in Grimshaw 1979 are not treated.

the Canonical Structural Realizations (or at least possible realizations) for the selected types (Grimshaw 1981 reprinted here as Chapter 3): the CSR of action is VP, of event is IP and of proposition is CP. Functional heads whose projections belong to different semantic types from their complements *appear* to be selected for, but in reality it is the type itself which is selected.

The striking prediction that this theory makes, then, is that if there are two complement structures of the same syntactic category and the same semantic type, *no predicate can choose between them*. In the remainder of this section I examine two instances of complementation which support this prediction.

Why is NegP invisible to selection? That is, why are higher heads never sensitive to the presence or absence of Neg? The type-category theory of selection answers this. First of all, Neg must form an extended verbal projection, so we know that its category is the same as that of other members of the verbal set, including TP. Thus no predicate could c-select NegP versus TP, or TP versus NegP, since NegP and TP are not distinguishable by category. Hence NegP is in effect invisible to c-selection. What of s-selection? Clearly Neg changes meaning, but it seems extremely plausible to suppose that it does not change semantic type – a negated proposition is still a proposition, a negated event is still an event and so forth. Suppose then that Neg is among the type-preserving heads. It follows that no higher head can semantically select for its presence or absence, since its presence or absence is not reflected in the type system. In sum, Neg is invisible to both c-selection (because of its category) and s-selection (because it is not type-changing).[41] Hence we derive the result that it is not selectable.

Two other instances of non-selectable alternatives are *for-to* versus *to* infinitives and IP versus CP with all bridge verbs. The verbs (and adjectives) which take *for-to* complements all take in addition, bare *to* infinitives[42]. The pattern is illustrated in (72).

(72) a.   We arranged (for them) to get free tickets.
      b.   We are eager (for them) to get free tickets.

---

[41] In the analysis of Basque given by Laka (1990), V can select for a negative C. This is consistent with the type-category theory of selection only if it is semantic selection that is involved, and the V is selecting a negative CP which is of a different semantic type from a non-negated CP. It would be surprising, however, if negative and positive CP differ in type, given that negative and positive IPs do not seem to. So this case needs to be re-examined from the perspective of type-category selection.

[42] The converse does not hold: verbs like *try* do not allow the *for-to* structure. This cannot be due to selection, under the present assumptions, but must be due to the relationship of obligatory control and its consequences.

If neither s-selection nor c-selection can distinguish between the two types of complement, the absence of arbitrary selection here is explained.

Similarly all "bridge verbs" (see Vikner 1995 for recent discussion) take both CP complements headed by *that* and IP complements. There are none that take only a finite IP and disallow the CP option. Those that take only CPs are recognized as belonging to a semantic subclass of "non-bridge" verbs.

(73)   Many people think (that) conditions in the stock market will improve.
        The chair told the faculty (that) they should teach more students.

Since there is no arbitrary variation among bridge verbs as to whether they take IP, CP, or both, we conclude that the choice is not a matter of selection, i.e. not under the control of individual verbs. This is as expected when the IPs and CPs concerned belong to the same semantic type as well as the same syntactic category. Of course if a complementizer signals a particular semantic type, such as interrogative, a predicate which selects for that type will, as a consequence, appear only with CP complements. This is not, however, a case of "selection for CP" but simply of selection for interrogative, with syntactic consequences. (There is therefore no argument from selection to posit a CP when C and its specifier position are both empty. These clauses can be analyzed as IPs and still satisfy the selection of the higher predicate. See Doherty 1993 and Grimshaw 1997.)

While it is commonplace to see the term "selection" used in characterizing the relationship between a functional head and its complement, I believe that this is essentially a terminological convention, rather than a substantive claim about the nature of functional heads or the nature of selectional relations. Extended Projection makes it possible to understand complements to F-heads quite differently, and clears the way to a significantly different view of the theory of selection.

1.7   Conclusion

There are many ways in which the idea of Extended Projection might be wrong. Perhaps functional heads really don't form a syntactic unit with their complements. Or perhaps they do form a unit, but it has nothing to do with syntactic category. And of course the specific proposals made here could be misguided. It could turn out that the behavior of functional heads and their complements is every bit as arbitrary as the "selection" hypothesis fundamentally predicts: any head can select for any complement. In this case there is no theory of the organization of functional projections and no point in trying to construct one. However, the research program that many syntacticians have been engaged in for almost twenty years is accumulating results suggestive of significant coherence in the domain of functional structure. This paper sets out one version of one kind of theory of this coherence.

APPENDIX
Extended Projection – an Annotated Bibliography

This appendix collects together a number of works which address central issues in the theory of extended projections or modify the theory. Since the draft of this paper first circulated in 1991, and since the publication of the closely related work by Henk van Riemsdijk, the term "extended projection" has entered the linguistic repertoire of the field. It is used frequently without commitment to the theory beyond the bare minimum, not to mention without attribution. I have limited the work included here to studies which concern the content of the theory itself, try to grapple with difficult aspects of it, and attempt to explore its consequences, for better or worse. I hope that the brief discussions provided here will enable the reader to follow up on outstanding issues of particular interest.

Bayer, J. 1996. *Directionality and Logical Form: On the scope of focusing particles and wh-in-situ.* Dordrecht: Kluwer.

Having argued that PPs are in general barriers in German, Bayer addresses the question of why PPs are not barriers when the object of the preposition is a wh-phrase or other kind of quantified DP. He notes that this can be explained in terms of specifier-head agreement and the percolation of a feature from one maximal projection to another within the same extended projection. See especially p. 111–116. Bayer additionally proposes a definition of a "Barrier," which utilizes extended projection. The goal is to explain why material can extract from NP into the specifier position of the dominating DP, and from there to a yet higher structural position. See especially p. 125.

Bayer, J. and A. Grosu. 2000. Feature Checking meets the criterion approach: three ways of saying *only* in Romance and Germanic. In V. Motapanyane ed. *Comparative studies in Romanian syntax*, 49–81. Amsterdam; New York: Elsevier.

The authors suggest an implementation of the categorial identity of lexical heads and the functional heads in their extended projection in terms of interpretable and uninterpretable features. For example, a lexical head N would carry an interpretable N feature, and the functional heads associated with it would carry an uninterpretable N feature, forcing the N feature of the lexical head to raise through the functional heads above it. They then draw on this idea in explaining why *only* cannot attach to the complement of a preposition in Italian, French, German and Romanian: if *only* has no categorical features it cannot participate in the raising sequence, hence can never reach the PP level and never attain a position appropriate for its scope.

Bittner, M. and K. Hale. 1996. The Structural Determination of Case and Agreement. *Linguistic Inquiry* 27:1–68.

This paper incorporates the idea of extended projection into a number of facets of the theory of case. Bittner and Hale propose that case ("K") is the highest head in a nominal extended projection, comparable to C in a verbal extended projection. Like Bayer 1996, Bittner and Hale incorporate extended projection into the definition of a "Barrier" (p. 11); they appeal to the categorial relationship between V and I in explicating the (historical) reanalysis of a lexical head into a functional category (p. 40); and they appeal to the parallel status of D in the nominal extended projection and I in the verbal extended projection in explaining why case patterns are sometimes shared between DPs and IPs (p. 60). They derive the fact that only lexical heads can assign inherent case (they count P as lexical), from the fact that maximal extended projections (those which include the highest possible level of functional structure) can occur only as complements to lexical heads.

Borsley, R. and J. Kornfilt. 2000. Mixed Extended Projections. In Robert Borsley ed. *The Nature and Function of Syntactic Categories*, 101–131. Syntax and Semantics 32. Academic Press.

The authors build on the idea that some functional projections are verbal and some nominal in an exploration of clausal constructions with nominal properties. They argue that such clausal constructions involve nominal functional projections occurring on top of a verbal lexical projection, with the possibility of verbal functional projections between the two, and they review a number of interesting cases which might be analyzed this way. (See also Zaring and Hirschbühler 1997.) Borsley and Kornfilt argue that the best analysis requires admitting "mixed" extended projections of the kind that I try to eliminate. (They consider several alternatives: positing two projections, positing a category neutral D, as for Deg in Grimshaw 1991, included here with some modifications as Chapter 1). They do not consider the analysis proposed in Grimshaw 1991 (and here), in which it is the suffix *-ing* that is category neutral.) It is difficult to see how to accept their conclusion without adopting a theory which allows all combinations of categories, or setting up a cumbersome set of stipulations governing which combinations of categories are possible and which not. This is why I have elected to preserve the strong form of the theory and look elsewhere for the special properties of apparently mixed constructions.

Büring, D. and K. Hartmann. 2001. The Syntax and Semantics of Focus-Sensitive Particles in German. *Natural Language and Linguistic Theory* 19:229–281.

Büring and Hartmann argue that focus particles in German can never attach to nominals; they are adverbials, which attach only to non-arguments. The focus adverbial must adjoin within the extended projection dominating the focused constituent, and to the closest maximal projection in that extended projection. See the final definition of the "Particle Theory" on p. 266. So if an indirect object is focused, the focus adverbial can in principle adjoin to the VP dominating the indirect object, the IP dominating that VP, and the CP dominating that IP. Since the VP is the lowest maximal projection which dominates the focus and is a non-argument, the focus adverbial adjoins to the VP and other adjunction sites are ungrammatical.

Cardinaletti, A. and G. Giusti. 2001. "Semi-lexical" motion verbs in Romance and Germanic. In Norbert Corver and Henk van Riemsdijk eds. *Semi-lexical categories*, 371–414. Mouton de Gruyter.

Cardinaletti and Giusti study motion verbs such as *go* in a variety of Romance and Germanic systems. They show that structures like *I went and bought bread* are mono-clausal, and that the motion verbs have many properties in common with auxiliaries. On the other hand, to varying degrees they retain some of the semantic content of lexical verbs. The authors conclude that these verbs are generated as part of the extended projection of the lexical head verb. This view is an alternative to the proposal of Vos (1999) and van Riemsdijk (1998) that there is a third type of head, which is "semi-lexical."

Cheng, L. 1995. On dou-quantification. *Journal of East Asian Linguistics* 4:197–234.

Cheng argues that *dou* "all" in Mandarin Chinese is an adverbial, which can adjoin to any member of the verbal extended projection: e.g. V^0, V', Asp^0, Asp'.

Chung, S. 1994. Wh-Agreement and "Referentiality" in Chamorro. *Linguistic Inquiry* 25:1–44.

Wh-agreement (i.e. agreement between an extracted wh phrase and some head in the verbal extended projection) provides evidence for patterns of long versus local wh-movement.

Cole, P., G. Hermon and L-M. Sung. 1993. Feature Percolation. *Journal of East Asian Linguistics* 2:91–118.

Exploring the consequences of general principles of feature index-percolation (if the features of mother and daughter nodes conflict, the mother node has the features of the head, otherwise mother and daughter nodes have identical features), Cole, Hermon and Sung observe a restriction: "No feature can percolate out of a lexical complement structure" (p. 110). They point out that this restriction reflects the role of extended projection in structure, since complements of lexical heads are not part of the extended projection of the head, and may be derived from the theory.

Corver, N. 1997a. The Internal Syntax of the Dutch Extended Adjectival Projection. *Natural Language and Linguistic Theory* 15:289–368.

As the title suggests, this paper investigates adjectives in Dutch, from a perspective which broadly assumes Extended Projection. Corver aims to establish that adjectives are lexical heads forming an extended projection with higher functional structure, and that there are three types of functional heads which participate, which he labels "Deg," "Q" and "Agr." Moreover, head-to-head movement occurs within the extended projection.

Corver, N. 1997b. *Much*-support as a last resort. *Linguistic Inquiry* 28:119–164.

The well-formedness of an adjectival extended projection can depend on the appearance of *much*, which appears as a "last resort" to allow *too* to bind a degree argument in *so*, in forms like *too much so*. The appearance of *much* with adjectives is thus analogous to the appearance of *do*-support in clauses.

Franks, S. 1994. Parametric Properties of Numeral Phrases in Slavic. *Natural Language and Linguistic Theory* 12:599–674.

Franks exploits Extended Projection in trying to explain patterns of case in numerically quantified phrases, particularly in Russian and Serbo-Croation. The spreading of case within structurally case-marked phrases in Russian, analyzed in early work of Leonard Babby's (see

Franks 1994 for references), motivates the view that functional phrases dominating lexical phrases share an index, allowing percolation of case features.

Fu, J., T. Roeper and H. Borer. 2001. The VP within process nominals: Evidence from adverbs and the VP anaphor *do so*. *Natural Language and Linguistic Theory* 19:549–582.

Process nominals are shown to allow certain adverbs, and argued to act as antecedents for *do so*. The authors conclude that the lower part of the VP extended projection (consisting of Asp_P and Asp_E) appears within process nominals, in the complement to a nominalizing affix. Whether this proposal is consistent with Extended Projection or not depends on the status of the verbal complement. If it is an extended projection distinct from the extended projection of the nominalizing affix, the proposed structure is consistent with Extended Projection, with each extended projection having the same syntactic category and a regular arrangement of functional structure. Otherwise, the structures are inconsistent with Extended Projection.

Ghomeshi, J. 1997. Non-projecting Nouns in Persian. *Natural Language and Linguistic Theory* 15:729–788.

Arguing that Persian nominals do not take phrasal complements or phrasal modifiers, Ghomeshi proposes that nouns do not project in Persian; they take neither specifiers nor complements. Instead, they combine with other X^0 level elements by adjunction. A vowel marks each nominal lexical head (nouns and some prepositions) which is non-final in the extended projection of the head noun, more precisely, which is followed by phonetically overt non-affixal material in the extended projection of the head noun.

Grosu, A. 1996. The Proper Analysis of "Missing-P" Free Relative Constructions. *Linguistic Inquiry* 27:257–293.

In elaborating an analysis for free relatives in general, and those with apparently missing prepositions in particular, Grosu draws the distinction between features which are inherent to an extended projection, and those which are inherited by one. Inherent features block the percolation of inherited features. By inheritance, features can be transmitted to heads and projections which never have them inherently. Grosu suggests that this lies behind the marginal status of free relatives with missing prepositions, where a PP must inherit, from a wh nominal, indices and phi-features which are not intrinsically associated with Ps and PPs.

Haeberli, E. 1998. Categorial Feature Matrices and Checking. In *Proceedings of the North East Linguistic Society* 28:77–93. University of Massachusetts, GLSA.

Haeberli, E. 2002. *Features, Categories and the Syntax of A-Positions.* Dordrecht: Kluwer.

With a modified version of the theory of categories hypothesized in Extended Projection and in van Riemsdijk 1990, Haeberli argues that abstract case theory and the EPP can both be reduced to checking theory.

Haegeman, L. 1995. *The Syntax of Negation.* Cambridge University Press.

Haegeman's fundamental hypothesis is that negative phrases must appear in a specifier-head relationship with a negative head. Since the phrase can be separated from the negative head, but must occur within the same extended projection, Haegeman proposes that the extended projection is the domain within which the criterion governing negatives is satisfied. In a related discussion of the syntax of A-positions, she addresses the issue of why a subject can move across an object, and an object across another object, within a single IP. She suggests that elements in the same extended projection are exempted from Relativized Minimality. See also Roberts 1997.

Josefsson, G. 1993. Scandinavian pronouns and object shift. *Working Papers in Scandinavian Syntax* 52:1–28. Department of Scandinavian Linguistics, Lund.

Swedish admits nominals in which a pronoun precedes the D, taking the DP as complement by hypothesis, and in effect "doubling" the DP. Josefsson proposes that the pronoun is present to spell out phi-features which the D does not encode overtly, such as animacy and gender. Since the pronoun is simply another functional head, it shares phi-features with every other head in the nominal extended projection.

Rafel, J. 2001. As for *as/for*, they are semi-lexical heads. In Norbert Corver and Henk van Riemsdijk eds. *Semi-lexical categories*, 475–503. Mouton de Gruyter.

Rafel analyzes the particles in examples like *They regard John as smart, They took John for a fool*, as the highest head of the extended projection of the predicate, here *smart* or *fool*. He argues that these particles have both lexical and functional characteristics.

Roberts, I. 1997. Restructuring, Head Movement and Locality. *Linguistic Inquiry* 28:423–460.

Roberts proposes that predicates which allow restructuring are those which form a single extended projection with their complement, as auxiliaries do with theirs, through incorporation. Under this analysis, the domain of long NP movement, auxiliary selection and clitic climbing is an extended projection: these effects are local despite appearances. Roberts modifies Relativized Minimality so that an element cannot block chain formation involving another element in the same extended projection; note 2 points out the interesting relationship between this account and "equidistance" (Chomsky 1993). See also Haegeman 1995 on Extended Projection and Relativized Minimality.

Tomioka, S. 1994. The Licensing of Lexical Projections. In E. Benedicto and J. Runner eds. *Functional Projections*, 209–226. University of Massachusetts Occasional Papers 17. Amherst, Massachusetts.

If a VP can occur as the complement to a V, as several recent analyses assert, what predicts the distribution and behavior of such inner VPs? Tomioka proposes that lexical projections must be either complements to functional heads, or complements to a lexical head into which incorporation occurs. He remarks that these can be viewed as alternative ways to form a single extended projection. Note that his discussion is relevant to the question raised in "Extended Projection" of whether two heads with the same F-value can combine into an extended projection.

Vikner, S. 1995. *Verb Movement and Expletive Subjects in the Germanic Languages.* New York; Oxford: Oxford University Press.

In analyzing the grammatical locations for adjunction in German, Vikner concludes that adjunction is possible to the highest member of the verbal extended projection: hence not to a VP within an IP, for example.

Zaring, L. and P. Hirschbühler. 1997. Qu'est-ce que *ce que*? The diachronic evolution of a French complementizer. In A. van Kemenade and N. Vincent eds. *Parameters of Morphosyntactic Change*, 351–379. Cambridge University Press.

Zaring and Hirschbühler analyze the sequence *ce que* in Old and Middle French, and conclude that it consists of a Det (*ce*) with a CP complement. (Cf. Borsley and Kornfilt 2000.) They recognize that this is inconsistent with the category matching requirement for an extended projection (assuming that these structures are in fact a single extended projection, rather than a combination of two). They also argue that the Det should not be considered category neutral, since the distribution of the entire phrase is not properly predicted by this analysis. They propose that the categorial identity requirement be parameterized, with the default setting requiring matching, and the learned setting allowing mis-matches. While this proposal does successfully treat categorially mixed extended projections as marked, it does not explain, as far as I can see, why such marked structures should not occur widely in a language with the marked setting. Once the parameter has been set to allow mixed extended projections, the language must allow them wherever they violate no other principle of grammar. It seems that in order to prevent this, the parameter would have to be interpreted as governing a particular functional head, or a particular configuration, rather than governing a general syntactic property of the linguistic system.

Zwarts, J. 1992. X′-Syntax – X′-Semantics: On the Interpretation of Functional and Lexical Heads. Doctoral dissertation. Rijksuniversiteit te Utrecht. OTS dissertation series.

Zwarts proposes an alternative to the conception of Extended Projection in Grimshaw 1991, and to the related proposals in van Riemsdijk 1990. He correctly points out that the hierarchical ordering of functional heads is simply stipulated by means of an F-value, and that we have therefore failed to explain why, for instance, complementizers appear outside the position of T. Zwarts proposes that lexical categories are "bundles of categorial features" and that functional categories are "bundles of grammatical features." The idea is then that the hierarchical structure of functional heads is determined by an ordering over the grammatical features; since this ordering is taken to be independently necessary, theoretical arbitrariness has been reduced. The status of this claim is not entirely clear. It seems that exactly the same point holds for the hierarchy of functional heads given in Section 1.5: the position of each head is stated only once, in terms of the hierarchy of functional specifications. It is unarguably the case, though, that none of these theories can be said to *explain* the hierarchical organization of functional features and/or heads. At best we have stipulated it only once.

Works Cited in Chapter 1

See References on page 129 for publication information on the following works cited in this chapter.

Abney 1987
Ackema 2001
Austin and Bresnan 1996
Baker 1988
Baker and Hale 1990
Baltin 1989, 1995
Bayer 1984, 1996
Bayer and Grosu 2000
Beerman 1990
Belletti 2001
Bennis and Haegeman 1984
Bhatt and Yoon 1992
Bittner and Hale 1996
Bobaljik and Jonas 1996
Borsley and Kornfilt 2000
Brame 1981, 1982
Bresnan and Mchombo 1987
Büring and Hartmann 2001
Cardinaletti and Giusti 2001
Cheng 1991, 1995
Chomsky 1970a, 1986a, 1993, 1995
Chung 1990, 1994
Chung and McCloskey 1987
Cinque 1990, 1994, 1999
Cole, Hermon and Sung 1993
Corver 1990, 1991, 1997a, 1997b
Cowper 1987
den Besten 1977
Doherty 1993, 1996, 1997
Dubinsky and Williams 1995
Emonds 1985
Fassi Fehri 1987
Finer 1997
Franks 1994
Fu, Roeper and Borer 2001

Fukui 1986
Fukui and Speas 1986
Georgopoulos 1987
Ghomeshi 1997
Giusti 1997
Grimshaw 1979, 1981, 1991, 1993,
    1997, 2000, 2001, 2003, (in prep)
Grosu 1996
Guéron and Hoekstra 1988
Haeberli 1998, 2001, 2002
Haegeman 1991, 1995
Haider 1988
Hellan 1985
Hestvik 1991
Holmberg 1986
Holmberg and Platzack 1995
Hornstein 1977
Jackendoff 1973, 1977
Josefsson 1993
Kathol 2000
Kayne 1997, 1998, 1999
Kim 1994
Koopman 1984
Koster 1978, 1985, 1987
Kratzer 1996
Laka 1990
Landau 2002
Larson 1988, 1990
Lefebvre and Massam 1988
Lefebvre and Muysken 1988
Li 1990
Longobardi 1994
McCloskey and Hale 1984
Muysken 1983
Nakajima 1991

Ouhalla 1990, 1997
Pesetksy 1982
Pesetsky and Torrego 2001
Plann 1986
Pollock 1989
Postal 1974
Potsdam 1997
Radford 1993
Rafel 2001
Reuland 1986
Ritter 1987, 1991
Rivero 2000
Rizzi 1990, 1997
Roberts 1997
Rochette 1990, 1998
Rosen 1989

Rosenbaum 1967
Ross 1967
Rothstein 1991
Schwarzschild 2002
Song 1988
Suñer 1991
Tomioka 1994
van Riemsdijk 1978, 1985, 1990,
    1998
Vikner 1995
Vos 1999
Zamparelli 2000
Zanuttini 1990, 1996, 1997
Zaring and Hirschbüler 1997
Zeller 2001
Zwarts 1992, 1995

2

Semantic Structure and Semantic Content in Lexical Representation

It is very easy to ask what a word means, and very hard to answer the question. One contributing factor is that the meaning of the verb *mean* is not at all clear, thus of *melt* or *freeze* in (1) it seems perfectly reasonable to say that it means that something happened, that it means that the ice-cream changed its state, that it means that someone caused the ice-cream to change its state, that someone did something, that the ice-cream became liquid (1a) or solid (1b), and so forth.

(1)   a.   He melted the ice-cream.

     b.   He froze the ice-cream.

Similarly for the pair in (2):

(2)   a.   She wrote a book.

     b.   She drew a picture.

Of (2) we can say that she did something, something existed after she did it, she used an instrument of some kind and so forth. Thus there are many different kinds of answers to the question of what *write* and *draw* mean, or what *melt* and *freeze* mean. The issue I am concerned with here is that of how this information is represented linguistically, i.e. in the grammatical system for morphemes.

    The argument I will make is that semantic properties of predicates divide into two fundamentally different kinds of information. I suggest that the division corresponds to the distinction between information that is linguistically analyzed and information that, while it may be cognitively analyzed, is linguistically atomic. The argument is based on the idea that some meaning components have a grammatical life, and some are linguistically inert. There is a sense in which this position is a distillation of a general research trend (see in particular Talmy

1985, Pinker 1989, Van Valin 1990, Levin and Rappaport Hovav 1991). Nevertheless in developing the idea we are led to an analysis which is sharply different from what most current work assumes. I will explore a very strong version of this position in which very little information is linguistically represented, and I will try to provide a fairly rich set of criteria which serve to delineate the two kinds of information.

To preview the conclusion, it will split the analysis of a verb like *write* in the following way: that *write* means to do something and not to be something is linguistic; that it means what it means and not what *draw* means, is not. Similarly, that *melt* and *freeze* both (can) mean to change state is linguistic, that they concern changes in liquidity, and that each means what it means and not what the other means is not: it is purely a matter of content. The aspect of meaning that distinguishes *write* from *draw*, or *melt* from *freeze* is of no linguistic significance and plays no role in the grammatical system of the language. It is, like the difference between *cat* and *dog*, *geographer* and *philosopher*, *concept* and *word*, a difference, perhaps even an important difference, but not a linguistic one.

The aspect of lexical meaning which is linguistically active I will call "semantic structure." The aspect of lexical meaning which is inactive linguistically I will call "semantic content" (cf. Grimshaw 1994, Pinker 1989, 1994). Thus *melt* and *freeze* have the same semantic structure, as do *write* and *draw*, *push* and *pull*, *sing* and *dance*. They have different semantic content, as do *dog* and *cat*. Semantic structure has linguistic life, semantic content does not.

Linguistically speaking pairs like these are synonyms, because they have the same structure. The differences between them are not visible to the language. In fact, what are usually thought of as antonyms are exactly of this type: they have the same semantic structure. In addition they have semantic content which meets certain constraints of semantic field and polarity. Structurally speaking they are synonyms, then, within the perspective argued for here, distinguished by semantic content. (Semantic field, of course, is a matter of semantic content, and cross-classifies with semantic structure.)

2.1   The Linguistic Life of Semantic Structure

2.1.1   Syntactic Expression

Semantic structure but not semantic content determines the syntactic expression of the arguments of a predicate. For example, change-of-state predicates are unaccusative, i.e. they have no external argument, and no deep structure subject. Examples include:

(3) a. The water cooled.

  b. The plant grew.

As has been shown over the past fifteen years, this has many and far-reaching grammatical consequences, see Levin and Rappaport Hovav 1995 for a recent review.

In contrast, activity predicates are unergative: they have an external argument.

(4) a. She shouted.

  b. He wrote.

This is just one example of how mapping from lexical semantics to syntactic structure works. The important point is that the mapping clearly depends on certain aspects of the semantics of the predicate and not others. Thus it is crucial whether the predicate is one of change-of-state or activity but not whether it concerns temperature or size. This is because the linguistically significant aspects of lexical meaning are highly limited in character, and only they can interact with the grammatical system in any way. Whether a predicate concerns size or temperature is linguistically invisible, since the distinction concerns content only.

If content and structure are distinct they have the potential to cross-classify. Thus we expect to find pairs with matched content, but different semantic structures. A candidate is the pair originally pointed out in Rosen 1984, and recently analyzed by Levin and Rappaport Hovav (1995): while *blush* in English behaves like an unergative, its Italian counterpart *arrossire* behaves like an unaccusative. Yet the two verbs appear to "mean the same thing," in some sense. Levin and Rappaport Hovav show that *arrossire* is really a change of state predicate and not an activity predicate, hence its unaccusativity is expected. From the present perspective, then, this is a case of more-or-less identical semantic content being mapped onto two alternative structures: the unaccusative change-of-state structure in Italian and the unergative structure in English. The existence of such examples provides strong support for the separation of content and structure.

Note that under this view, the two verbs mean the same thing only in a pre-theoretic sense, which can be roughly analyzed as denoting the same events. Clearly this pre-theoretic notion is quite different from the notion of verbal meaning that is the topic of this paper.

Of course there may sometimes be a relationship between semantic structure and semantic content: a certain content might naturally lend itself to expression in a particular range of structures. E.g. a predicate pertaining to heat might typically occur in causative and change-of-state structures, while one pertaining to calculation presumably will not.

2.1.2   Applicability of Linguistic Operations

Semantic structure determines the possibility of linguistic operations. Semantic content does not. For example, it is possible to form a passive from a verb with particular semantic structure properties – technically those which result in the verb having an external argument (see Grimshaw 1990 for discussion). A verb with no external argument does not passivize. Hence we find contrasts like the one in (5).

(5)   a.   The professor was shot by her students.

b.   *The professor was resembled by her students.

In contrast, no such generalizations hold for content. There is no morpheme which passivizes all verbs having to do with colour: *paint, colour, bleach, redden, stain.* Or which passivizes verbs that have to do with heat but not cold (*melt, boil, heat* but not *freeze, cool, chill*). This is because information of this kind is not part of the linguistic representation of a morpheme, hence it is invisible to linguistic processes. In particular it cannot interact with the linguistic representation of another morpheme, while information about the external status of an argument can, and does.

In fact, the history of the exploration of these operations has often involved a shift from an early position which we can describe as content-based to a theoretically and empirically sharper structural hypothesis. The eventual hypothesis, then, is consistent with the claim that the applicability of grammatical operations like these is determined by semantic structure and is totally insensitive to semantic content.

2.1.3   Effects of Linguistic Operations

By the same token, the effects of linguistic operations are structural in nature, and they do not change content. (Under the particular assumptions I make here the only linguistic operations that affect the internal analysis of words are those that combine morphemes. However, the general argument still holds under a less strict theory of the lexicon, so I will not pursue this issue.) A simple example is the addition of a morpheme like English *-en*: *red* becomes *redden*. The semantic structure changes, from a state to a caused-change-of-state or a change-of-state. The content, however, remains unchanged.

Similarly, when a single predicate occurs in a wide range of different configurations, the content is maintained in each case, while the structure varies.

(6)   a.   The water is cool.
      b.   The water cooled.
      c.   They cooled the water.

The morpheme is associated with a fixed content, while the structure varies (for present purposes it doesn't matter exactly what the right treatment of the semantic structure variation is).

2.1.4   Cross Linguistic Variation

Since Talmy 1985 it has been recognized that there is systematic cross-linguistic variation in the ways in which morpheme meanings can be composed. Talmy pointed out that verbs like *float* in English can simultaneously express manner and motion (*The ball floated into the cave*) while in French such a verb is not possible. The counterpart verb can only express manner. Thus there are differences in the set of possible semantic structures for French and English. On the other hand there are no such differences in the set of possible semantic contents for French and English. They may have different actual contents but not different possible contents.

Systematic cross-linguistic variation in lexical structure is just like systematic cross-linguistic variation in any other part of language: it reflects the varying options admitted by Universal Grammar. (See Choi and Bowerman 1991 for a relevant acquisition study.) But Universal Grammar does not constrain lexical content, hence variation in lexical content does not have the profile familiar from the truly linguistic domains.

2.1.5   Selectional Restrictions

Predicates impose semantic restrictions on the items they enter into construction with by means of what is sometimes called "selection." However, it turns out that these restrictions fall into two classes. One is based on semantic content and hence is entirely non-linguistic. Sentences which violate this class are strange but they are strange for non-linguistic reasons. Consider for example, the cases in (7):

(7)   a.   He drank the meat/car/universe.
      b.   He sliced the orange juice.

It is true that we cannot in fact drink things that are not drinkable or slice things that are not sliceable, but this has nothing to do with the ability of the verb to take one kind of NP complement or another. Clear evidence for this comes from a comparison between (7) and (8), where the same verbs occur with the same direct objects in perfectly normal sentences (cf. Horn 1989 on effects of negation here):

(8)   a.   Noone can drink meat/cars/the universe.

       b.   It isn't possible to slice orange juice.

The difference is that the sentences in (7) assert that a highly unlikely or impossible event occurred, while those in (8) assert that such an event is unlikely or impossible. There is nothing wrong with combining *slice* and *orange juice*, then, although it is quite odd to claim that an event of orange juice slicing has occurred. The same general point holds of *Colorless green ideas sleep furiously* (Chomsky 1957).

In contrast, there are other semantic restrictions, (distinguished from syntactic restrictions in Grimshaw 1979), which are linguistic in character, and pertain to the semantic structure of the predicate.

(9)   a.   I think that he is here.

       b. #I think whether he is here.

       c. #I drank that he is here.

These verb-complement combinations contrast with those just cited precisely in that the manipulations illustrated in (10) make no difference.

(10)   a. #Noone can think whether he is here.

        b. #It isn't possible to drink that he is here.

When the verb takes the wrong kind of sentential complement there is something wrong with the sentence, not just with the event the sentence describes. Hence even sentences which deny the possibility of the event are ill-formed.

The conclusion, then, is that there are restrictions based on semantic content which concern possible events, states etc., and are non-linguistic in character. Then there are restrictions based on the truly linguistic properties of a predicate, its semantic structure, and these are linguistic in character. (I have to leave open the issue of exactly what aspect of semantic structure governs complement selection of this type. Baker 1968 contains some important ideas about interrogatives.) Again, then, semantic content splits off sharply from the grammatically relevant aspects of lexical meaning.

2.1.6 Content arguments and Structure Arguments

Comparing a pair of verbs such as a causative like *melt* and a transitive activity predicate like *study* we find an interesting difference in the status of the object arguments. While it is clear that the object of a

verb like transitive *melt* figures in the verb's semantic structure, since
it is the argument of a change-of-state predicate, it is much less clear
that the object of *study* is an argument by virtue of the structure
of the predicate. Rather it seems plausible that the structure simply
involves an activity, and it is the content of the activity that determines
that it can involve another argument. Let us then surmise that there
is indeed such a distinction, and label arguments that are present by
virtue of semantic structure "structure arguments" and arguments that
are present by virtue of semantic content "content arguments." (Beth
Levin points out (p.c.) that this distinction may ultimately be the same
as that encoded as presence or absence of a macro-role in Van Valin
1990.) The second argument of *study* then, is a content argument, in
contrast with the second argument of *melt*.

(11) a. *study* (x   (y))
$$|$$
x acts

b. *melt* (x   (y))
$$|\qquad\quad|$$
x causes   y changes state

The number of arguments a predicate actually takes depends, in
this view, not only on its semantic structure but also on its semantic
content. All activity predicates have the same semantic structure, yet
some are monadic, some are dyadic.

Of course, this theoretical move might be incorrect, if it turns out
that all arguments are present by virtue of semantic structure: this view
is certainly much closer to what standard assumptions would suggest
when grafted onto the structure/content distinction. However, I would
like to explore the possibility that arguments split up in this way and
point to three possible consequences.

First, the content argument/structure argument distinction sheds
some light on a long-standing problem of lexical semantics, most recently addressed in Dowty 1991. The theory of thematic roles provides
thematic labels in many cases with considerable clarity. For example,
there is no problem in deciding how to classify the subject argument of
either transitive *melt* or *study*: both are assigned the same label, and
it is the one that actors get in the system, say Agent, or Actor (see e.g.
Jackendoff 1990, Van Valin 1990). Of course there are various views
about the right system and so forth but it is clear that there is a right
system and that these arguments participate in it. The same holds for
the object of a causative predicate: it should be given the same label as

the subject of a corresponding change-of-state predicate and the same label as the object of all other causative predicates. Again, we can argue over various aspects of the analysis but it is clear that we are playing the right game in the right ballpark.

In contrast there are many arguments whose classification is entirely mysterious. What is the object of *study*, for example? Is it the same as or different from the object of *see* or *eat*? Such questions have proved extremely hard to answer. (The common practice of labeling otherwise unclassifiable arguments as Themes is a reflection of the fact that the problem is unsolved.) This suggests then that the idea of a thematic role label just does not extend to all arguments. In terms of the ideas under discussion, this would not be surprising if the thematic role system applies to structure arguments and not to content arguments.

We should abandon the assumption, then, that every argument can and should be assigned a thematic role label. Thematic role labels are, in this view, nothing more than labels for positions in semantic structure. Hence it is necessarily the case that we can sensibly label structure arguments and that the system breaks down with content arguments. The failure of any given system of thematic role labels to be effective at predicting linguistic properties of arguments is due, not to the fundamental failure of the enterprise, but to failure to respect the structure-content distinction.

Second, although this is a very hard point to establish empirically, the two kinds of argument seem to differ in their obligatoriness. In the pair of verbs we are examining, for example, the object of *study* is omissible, while that of *melt* must be expressed, thus (12b) is ungrammatical with a causative meaning, and can only have a change-of-state interpretation. This is why there is no possible interpretation for (12c).

(12)   a.   She studied.

       b.   The machine melted.

       c.   *The heat melted.

The observational optionality of certain arguments is still not well understood, and in order to purse this proposal further it will be necessary to make some important further distinctions. "Missing" arguments may be present lexically (i.e. incorporated), or may be elliptical, i.e. contextually present, for example.

However, a reasonable approximation of the situation is that structure arguments are always obligatory, while content arguments are omissible in principle. Optional arguments, then, are always content arguments. However, content arguments may not always be optional if other factors, such as the inherent transitivity of a verb, however expressed, can result in obligatory expression. For now, then, the clear prediction is that structure arguments are obligatory. This certainly appears to be correct for causative predicates, which are strongly transitive as a group, just like *melt* in (12).

This hypothesis promises an explanation for paradigms like the one in (13) and (14), where *write* and *draw* take objects optionally when they occur with the aspect-governed PP introduced by *for*, but obligatorily when they occur with the aspect-governed PP introduced by *in*.

(13)   a.   She wrote (letters) for an hour.

      b.   She wrote a letter in an hour.

      c.   *She wrote in an hour.

(14)   a.   She drew (a picture) for an hour.

      b.   She drew a picture in an hour.

      c.   *She drew in an hour.

The line of explanation is this. When these clauses have activity interpretations, as in (13a) and (14a), the object argument is only a content argument, hence it is optional. When they have telic interpretations as in (14), the object argument is a structure argument, being the subject of a predicate of coming-into-existence (see Dowty 1991), hence the argument is obligatory. Thus patterns like (13) and (14) fall into place.

The final point regarding structure arguments and content arguments concerns a long-standing puzzle in lexical research; the apparent significance of some notion like "affectedness" (Anderson 1979, Zubizarreta 1987, Giorgi and Longobardi 1991, Tenny 1992). The observation is that only affected arguments seem to be able to undergo certain processes such as "preposing" in nominals, and middle formation.

With the recognition of the importance of aspectual analysis for lexical representation has come the recognition that the notion of an affected argument corresponds to an aspectual notion, closely allied to undergoing a change of state.[1]

This solves part of the problem of what affectedness is, but why should it matter? The present proposal offers an answer to this ques-

---

[1]Like the notion "causative" discussed below, the relevant notion of affected argument pertains strictly to the lexical semantics of a predicate, not to events in the world. In an event of eating, both the eater and the eaten are affected in a certain sense: they are different before the event and after the event. Nevertheless neither of the two linguistic arguments of *eat* is affected in the linguistic sense of the term. (Here I differ from Zubizarreta (1987) who analyzed *eat* as having an affected object.)

tion. An affected argument is a structure argument. An unaffected argument is a content argument. Now suppose that structure arguments are visible to lexical operations: content arguments are invisible. Hence unaffected arguments are invisible. Thus no lexical operation could in principle implicate an unaffected argument since it will be invisible for such operations. Of course syntactic operations can apply to an unaffected argument since it is syntactically indistinguishable from any other direct object.

There is an alternative approach which could be taken here. The claim that unaffected arguments are not structure arguments makes it possible to explain the constraint proposed by Jaeggli (1986: 207). He suggested that the external argument of a predicate cannot be eliminated if the internal argument is unaffected. Thus predicates with unaffected arguments cannot undergo middle formation or preposing in nominals because, in these configurations, their external argument is not syntactically realized. Now, why should such a constraint hold? An answer could be proposed in the present theory: eliminating the external argument of a predicate with an unaffected object leaves the predicate with no structure argument. Suppose, then, that there is a well-formedness condition requiring every predicate to have at least one structure argument, then Jaeggli's generalization would follow. In this way we could provide a slightly different account of affectedness effects. This account also, of course, depends crucially on the idea that not every argument is a structure argument, and that unaffected arguments in particular are content arguments only.

In concluding, I will note that there is a clear prediction here: those arguments which qualify as affected should be obligatory. The two characteristics should coincide in this way since an affected argument must be a structure argument and structure arguments are obligatory. This is clearly correct for objects of causative predicates; further work is required to determine whether it holds more generally.

In the interests of clarity, let me make it clear that the content versus structure argument distinction is a lexical one: in terms of syntactic structure both kinds of argument behave in the same way. Hence they both undergo NP movement in passives and their extraction patterns are the same. Once they are projected into syntactic structure, then, the two kinds of arguments are of equal status. Lexically however, they are crucially distinct.

2.1.7 Lexical Complexity

How complicated can a verb meaning be? On the one hand it seems that the answer is: as complicated as you want. For example, suppose there is a manufacturing process that involves pulverizing something then mixing it with molten plastic, allowing it to harden and then encasing it in steel. Of course we can label the entire process with one verb: to *smolt*, for example.

However, looked at from another point of view, such a verb is semantically no more complex than any other: it is either a causative or an activity predicate.

What this suggests, then, is that it is true both that meanings can be of arbitrary complexity and that their complexity is highly limited. More precisely, in semantic content they can be of unlimited complexity, but in semantic structure they are rigidly constrained and must fall within the set of good semantic structures, which provide templates for good lexical meanings.

2.2 Other Views

The debate about how much structure there is in lexical items is an old one. Many current ideas about the question seem to assume a division roughly where I am arguing for it. For example, Baker (1988) argues that some word-internal derivational structure is syntactically represented. It seems, however, as though only semantic structure is at issue; work in this vein never proposes an analysis of semantic content, so we could view it in present terms as about the question of whether structure below the word level is just like structure above the word level, presupposing the structure/content distinction.

In contrast, a variety of other positions clearly conflict with the present proposal. I will consider the extremes. At one extreme much more of lexical meaning is linguistically analyzed. At the other extreme much less (perhaps none) of lexical meaning is linguistically analyzed.

To exemplify the much-analysis position we can consider the representation of *eat* given in Jackendoff 1990 (p. 253):

(15) $[\text{CAUSE} ([_{\text{Thing}}]^\alpha {}_{\text{A}'} [\text{GO} ([_{\text{Thing}}] {}_{<\text{A}>'}$
$[\text{TO} [\text{IN} [\text{MOUTH-OF} [\alpha]]]])])]$

Pretheoretically, this may represent what *eat* "means," but the representation differs from those suggested here in a couple of important respects.

First, *eat* is represented as a causative predicate. This leaves unexplained why *eat*, and all verbs like it, lack an inchoative form, while causative verbs in general have one:

(16) a. The girl ate the meal.

      b. *The meal ate.

(17) a. The girl melted the ice.

      b. The ice melted.

This strongly suggests that the linguistic representation of such a verb does not treat it as a causative. What imparts a causative flavour to the verb is not its lexical representation but the kind of event that it typically describes; in eating it is at least usually the case that one causes the food to enter the digestive system. I would argue, however, that this is a fact about the (canonical) event of eating and not about the linguistic representation of the verb.

The second key difference, more tightly connected to the present paper, is that the representation of *eat* in (15) does not distinguish semantic structure from semantic content. Given the arguments here, the difference between *eat* and *drink* is one which has no linguistic status: *eat* and *drink* are synonymous with respect to the language. Thus information about the liquidity of the intake is not part of the linguistic representation, and indeed nor is the information that the path involves the mouth. All of this is information about the concept of eating, and perhaps has an analysis, but if so it is a cognitive and not a linguistic one.

At the other extreme from Jackendoff's work is the position taken by Fodor (1970), Fodor et al. (1980) in which it is argued that there is no "lexical decomposition," i.e. internal semantic analysis for predicates, which are instead all atomic. Fodor (1970) presented several arguments which did indeed argue against the version of lexical decomposition which was at issue at the time. However, they are entirely consistent with the current theory, as I will now try to show. The essential point is that the existence of a lexical semantic analysis of a morpheme does not imply that it will have properties identical to those of a phrase or clause with a related meaning (for some related observations see Jackendoff 1990: 150–151 on lexical versus periphrastic causatives).

The issue Fodor addressed was whether the sentence *x caused y to die* is derived from the same d-structure as the sentence *x killed y*. The evidence showed that this was indeed not the right analysis. However, in current terms this is not the right question. The question is whether *kill* or *melt* has internal lexical structure. In the present theory, *kill* is a single morpheme and a lexical item, while *cause to die* is a piece of clausal structure. It follows from this that *kill* is subject to the well-formedness conditions that hold of single morphemes, while *cause to die* is subject not to these but to the well-formedness conditions that hold of syntactic structure.

Suppose, then, that single morphemes are subject to a condition that they must have a single event structure associated with them: for example, a given morpheme may have only one Actor argument, and only one temporal specification. Evidence for the one-Actor constraint comes from morphologically simple causatives, which only have "direct causation"meanings. They cannot mean "to cause some entity to act upon some other entity": *dress* does not and could not mean to cause someone to put on their clothes.

This is a property of single morpheme causatives, not of causatives in general, so periphrastic causatives, such as *cause to dress* obviously do not have this limitation, and neither do morphologically complex causatives.

Why should such a constraint hold? The answer is that single morphemes are forced to conform to the requirements of the lexical semantic template system, which admits only a limited set of possible semantic structures, all of which have to correspond to a single event. To put it another way, all of a verb's meaning must be bundled up in such a way that it is treated as denoting a single event.

This then provides the answer to the puzzle posed by Fodor (1970). If *kill* has causative structure then why doesn't it have the same properties as a clause with the same meaning? For example, why isn't it possible to have multiple temporal adverbials with *kill*, as it is with the corresponding periphrastic causative?

(18) a. I caused him to die on Tuesday by giving him poison on Monday.

      b. *I killed him on Tuesday by giving him poison on Monday.

The answer is that *kill* is a morpheme therefore it denotes a single event, and each event can have one temporal location. The phrase *cause to die*, on the other hand, is composed of two events, each of which has its own temporal location. In this way, some current ideas and results of lexical research explain the effects which Fodor took to show that lexical decomposition is incorrect.

2.3 Extensions and Implications

The general picture that emerges from these considerations is like this: only part of what we might pretheoretically describe as the "meaning" of a predicate is linguistically active. The idea explored in this paper is that the active part of a lexical meaning corresponds to that which is represented in lexical semantic structure. The result is that all predicates with the same semantic structure pattern together linguistically, regardless of differences in semantic content.

The argument here has been focussed on verbs, so what of nouns? A likely outcome of running through the same argument for nouns is that a distinction like the mass-count contrast would be properly analyzed as one of semantic structure. Thus *chairs and furniture* would have almost identical semantic content, but different semantic structure. As previously mentioned, nouns like *dog*, *cat* and *linguist* would probably be indistinguishable in semantic structure. The complex event nominals analyzed in Grimshaw 1990 would be analyzed like the corresponding verbs: their representation includes the semantic structure and event structure of the verbs they are based on. The line of reasoning extends to other categories too: it seems likely that the fact that a preposition is spatial might be a matter of semantic structure and hence correspond to a linguistically active property, while the fact that the preposition expresses a particular spatial relation rather than another one may be a matter of content only.

The final comment concerns the acquisition of the lexicon. There are two general ideas about how the lexicon is learned. One, which has become known as "semantic bootstrapping," is that from the semantics of a morpheme its syntax can be determined, modulo cross-linguistic variation in syntax of course (Grimshaw 1981, 1994, Pinker 1984, 1989, 1994). The other is that from the syntax of a morpheme its semantics can be, in part at least, determined (Gleitman 1990, Fisher, et al. 1991, Fisher et al. 1994). The argument of the present paper, if correct, establishes that both of these ideas about learning bear on the learning of semantic structure and/or lexical syntax. They can have no bearing on the acquisition of semantic content since this is not related to lexical syntax.

More generally, it seems that the two kinds of information, structure and content, must of necessity be learned quite differently. The learning of semantic content must be governed by a system quite different in character from those involved in linguistic learning: no theory of linguistic representation can be of help here. Observation about the world, and observation about the arguments of a predicate (*freeze* takes liquids as arguments, *melt* doesn't) must play a crucial role in the acquisition of semantic content. In the case of semantic structure, however, we expect the acquisition process to be of the same kind as that responsible for other linguistic systems, with the typical developmental and end-state patterns resulting from UG-constrained representation.

Works Cited in Chapter 2

See References on page 129 for publication information on the following works cited in this chapter.

Anderson 1979

Baker 1968

Baker 1988

Choi and Bowerman 1991

Chomsky 1957

Dowty 1991

Fisher, Gleitman and Gleitman 1991

Fisher, Hall Rackowitz and
    Gleitman 1994

Fodor 1970

Fodor, Garrett, Walker and Parkes
    1980

Giorgi and Longobardi 1991

Gleitman 1990

Grimshaw 1979, 1981, 1990, 1994

Horn 1989

Jackendoff 1990

Jaeggli 1986

Levin and Rappaport Hovav 1991,
    1995

Pinker 1984, 1989, 1994

Rosen 1984

Talmy 1985

Tenny 1992

Van Valin 1990

Zubizarreta 1987

3

Form, Function and the Language Acquisition Device [1]

I take the logical problem of language acquisition to be the problem of achieving explanatory adequacy in the sense established by Chomsky (e.g. 1965, 1970b). The task is to predict what grammar a learner will internalize as a function of the data available. The depth and complexity of the problem are well established (e.g. Peters 1972; Baker 1979).

The set of data available to the learner is highly limited in character; its single most problematic property is the absence of negative evidence – evidence that certain sentences are ill-formed. Given this, the theory of acquisition must guarantee that the language acquisition device (LAD) will either be right every time or will be wrong in such a way that positive evidence (plus whatever negative information is accessible) will suffice to justify the appropriate changes in the grammar.

By and large, the burden of providing this characterization of the acquisition process has been assumed by linguists to fall squarely on universal grammar, which consists of a *theory of grammatical representation* (TGR) plus an *evaluation metric* (EM). The working hypothesis of researchers has been that the logical problem of acquisition is reducible to the problem of constructing the right theory of universal grammar (UG). This gives rise to the familiar model of LAD in (1). [2]

---

[1] The concept of "canonical structural realization" or "CSR" introduced here is often attributed to Chomsky 1986b: 87–90. This is because Chomsky, while citing the present paper in footnote 35, does not mention that it is the source of canonical structural realization.

[2] "G_1" in (1) and (2) stands for the grammar (or perhaps more realistically the set of grammars) selected by the evaluation metric.

(1)

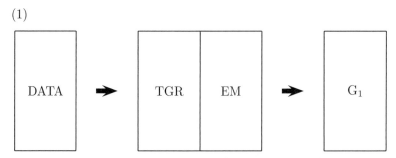

So if only we knew what UG in (1) stands for, we would know what LAD looks like.

I want to address two particular questions concerning (1). First, what is the nature of the evaluation metric? Is selection among grammars accomplished on purely formal grounds (e.g. by symbol counting) or do substantive criteria play a role? A hypothetical example may clarify the kind of evaluation metric I have in mind. Chomsky and Lasnik (1977) and Baker (1979) have noted that obligatory rules pose a problem for language learning. If linguistic theory permits a given rule to be either optional or obligatory, LAD needs evidence to decide between the two for each rule. But to learn that a rule is obligatory, it is necessary to have access to negative evidence – to know that sentences in which the rule does not apply are ungrammatical. The evaluation metric does not seem to determine the choice. In sum, LAD could never learn that a rule is obligatory. Therefore, grammars that include obligatory and optional rules are unlearnable.

The suggested remedy is this: linguistic theory must be restricted to disallow obligatory rules. (Of course the same result would be obtained if optional rules were disallowed.) This conclusion is, in my opinion, correct. However, it is not the only one possible. Suppose that LAD made the assumption that a rule is obligatory unless there were evidence for its optionality. Then LAD could learn the offending grammars with only positive evidence. If LAD heard a sentence in which a rule could have applied but didn't, the first hypothesis would be discarded, giving the rule optional status. Otherwise the rule would remain obligatory.

In this hypothetical case, the theory of grammatical representation simply says that rules can be optional or obligatory, but the evaluation metric assigns them a ranking in which obligatoriness has prior status. In effect, the fact that LAD exploits the proposed evaluation metric makes it possible for LAD to learn the grammars that are permitted by the theory of grammatical representation on the basis of the available evidence.

This leads to the second issue raised by (1). If the construction or evaluation of grammars is partly dependent upon substantive criteria, are the criteria always a matter of UG, or do nonlinguistic criteria play a significant role? The projection problem cannot be solved without the right theory of UG, but is UG sufficient? In formulating and evaluating grammars LAD may make use of a set of principles that pertain not to the theory of grammatical representation or an evaluation metric, but to the wider cognitive domain. In this case, the choice of hypotheses would not be linguistically determined but would be a function of UG plus properties of the child's general cognitive capacity. LAD equipped with linguistic theory, even the best linguistic theory, may be a failure at language acquisition.

If this is true, (1) must be revised to include reference to the child's cognitive capacity (CC), giving the model portrayed roughly in (2).

(2)

| DATA | → | TGR / CC | EM | → | G_1 |

The model in (2) is of course the model assumed in studies of language development (as opposed to learnability). To explain how child language changes over time it is clearly necessary to understand the child's developing cognitive abilities. The issue is whether resolution of the projection problem, which abstracts away from developmental data, also depends on the interaction of LAD's cognitive and linguistic capacities.

I want to take a particular aspect of UG, which I think is correct at least in essentials, and explore its implications for these two questions. The property of UG that I will focus on is the autonomy of syntax (Chomsky 1975). The linguistic motivation for the autonomy thesis is beyond the scope of this paper, but in the next section I will provide evidence from learnability which supports the theory.

I will argue that LAD can acquire grammars only by making use of a substantive evaluation metric relating form and function, and only by drawing on prelinguistic cognitive categorizations of the data. This study thus motivates the model in (2).

3.1 The Autonomy of Syntax and the Acquisition of Contextual Restrictions

It is a consequence of the autonomy of syntax that syntactic form and semantic type will not be in one-to-one correspondence in any principled way. A given syntactic form, such as NP or S, may correspond to a range of semantic types, and a given semantic type may have a number of alternative grammatical realizations. The implication for the acquisition of language is clear: UG does not permit deduction of a syntactic analysis from an analysis of the semantics of a phrase, and of course the same point holds for categorization of words. Thus the child must learn the two kinds of information separately; he must figure out what a word or phrase means, and what its syntax is.

Let me start by giving an illustration of how an autonomous system can be acquired. In the theory of contextual restrictions proposed in Grimshaw 1977, 1979, requirements imposed by predicates on their complements are expressed in terms of autonomous syntactic and semantic contextual restrictions. Predicates are subcategorized for the syntactic category – NP, S', etc., of their complements in the normal fashion. They select for the semantic type of their complements. Selection for indirect questions is represented by $<\_\_\_Q>$, for exclamatory complements by $<\_\_\_E>$ and for *that* complements by $<\_\_\_P>$ (P for "proposition"). Subcategorization is checked over syntactic representation, selection over semantic representation.

How is a lexical entry learned? Consider, for example, the entry for *know* given in (3). *Know* is subcategorized for NP and S', and it selects P, Q, and E.

$$(3) \quad know \quad [\_\_\_ \begin{Bmatrix} S' \\ NP \end{Bmatrix}] \quad <\_\_\_ \begin{Bmatrix} P \\ Q \\ E \end{Bmatrix}>$$

To learn this entry, five pieces of information are required. Does it take NP, S', P, Q, E? Three sentences will suffice:

(4) a. I know the answer $\quad\quad [\_\_\_NP] \; <\_\_\_Q>$
     b. I know what a fool he is $\quad [\_\_\_S'] \; <\_\_\_E>$
     c. I know that he is here $\quad\quad [\_\_\_S'] \; <\_\_\_P>$

This contrasts with the situation under a nonautonomous representation, where the syntactic form and the semantic type of a complement are encoded in a single representation. The entry for *know* in this theory would be something like (5):

(5)   *know* $\left[\begin{array}{c}\underline{\quad}\end{array}\left\{\begin{array}{c}\text{S}'/\text{P}\\\text{S}'/\text{Q}\\\text{S}'/\text{E}\\\text{NP}/\text{P}\\\text{NP}/\text{Q}\\\text{NP}/\text{E}\end{array}\right\}\right]$

Clearly the examples in (4) are insufficient for the acquisition of this entry (as is any other triple of sentences). From (4) LAD could deduce [___NP/Q], [___S'/E], and [___S'/P], but three additional cases are needed for completion of the entry.

When one considers also the possibility of Null Complement Anaphora – whether the complements of the verb are syntactically omissible or not – a similar point emerges. Given the autonomous representation, any one example of Null Complement Anaphora will motivate parentheses around S' (or, equivalently, around NP or around both).[3,4]

(6)   Did he leave? I don't know.

(7)   *know:* $\left[\begin{array}{c}\underline{\quad}\end{array}\left\{\begin{array}{c}(\text{S}')\\\text{NP}\end{array}\right\}\right]$

In the nonautonomous theory, this example will motivate parentheses around S'/Q but not around S'/P or S'/E. Two further examples are required:

(8)   a.   What a fool he is! I know.

      b.   He left. I know.

The key difference is that in the autonomous representation LAD has to learn only once that a predicate takes NP, that it takes Q, and so on. The combinatorial possibilities are a consequence of the representation and need not be learned at all. In the nonautonomous representation, LAD has to learn each possibility separately.

In general if there are n bits of syntactic information to be acquired, and m bits of semantic information, $n+m$ bits of evidence are needed for learning in the autonomous theory, nm in the nonautonomous theory.[5] In the case under discussion, $n = 3$ (does the predicate take NP, does it take S', and are they optional?), and $m = 3$ (does it take P, Q, E?). So it takes 6 bits of evidence to learn the entry for *know* given autonomy,

---

[3]Presumably a subcategorized phrase is assumed to be obligatory unless evidence for its optionality is received.

[4]Note that in fact (6) would also suffice to motivate <___P>, so (4a) and (4b) plus (6) would together provide all the evidence necessary for the complete lexical entry.

[5]For this formulation, thanks are due to Steve Pinker.

9 bits otherwise.

Thus the autonomy of syntax makes language learning easier, not harder. This is, of course, a paradigm case of the consequences of UG for learnability.

3.2 Form and Function

So it follows from the theory of grammatical representation that form and function (or type) cannot be expected to correspond in any pre-determinable or principled way. Nevertheless, I think there is reason to believe that LAD may rank grammars with a form-function correspondence over grammars that do not display one. I will discuss two cases where this seems to be true: with an evaluation metric to this effect, LAD will construct the correct grammar on the basis of the accessible data; without the evaluation metric the correct grammar is unlearnable, or at least no more highly valued than a number of incorrect alternatives.

3.3 Syntactic Rules

Consider the plight of LAD attempting to learn the grammar of matrix exclamations and non-echo wh questions.

(9) a. How tall has he grown?
     b. *Has he grown how tall?
     c. *How tall he has grown?

(10) a. How tall he has grown!
     b. *Has he grown how tall!
     c. *How tall has he grown!

LAD must learn that the (b) and (c) examples are ill-formed. This amounts to learning that wh-fronting must apply in both questions and exclamations, and that subject-auxiliary inversion must apply in questions and cannot apply in exclamations. The only evidence LAD has access to is that (9a) is a well-formed question, and that (10a) is a well-formed exclamation. Let us call the grammar that has (9) and (10) as consequences the "target grammar."

The question is, can LAD deduce the target grammar from UG plus the data? UG makes two relevant statements:

(11) (i) All rules are optional.[6]

    (ii) Form and function are independent.

Given this knowledge, LAD apparently has no reason to choose the target grammar over alternatives that would generate the (b) and (c) sentences.

Would a formal evaluation metric enable LAD to select the target grammar? Presumably it would, if the interpretation rules in the target grammar were simpler (or more highly valued in some way) than the interpretation rules in the alternative. There are two possibilities. First, the syntactic configurations in (b) and (c) simply might not be interpreted at all by the best set of projection and composition rules. But this is obviously not true – all the starred configurations in (9) and (10) correspond to grammatical, interpretable sentences. (9c) and (10c) are the same in form as (10a) and (9a) respectively, and the (b) cases are well-formed echo questions. So the projection rules will automatically interpret all the configurations.[7]

The second possibility is that rules which assign functions (like question, exclamation, declarative) to syntactic forms might be simpler in the target grammar than in the others. Suppose, for example, that the rules for the target grammar are those in (12):[8]

(12) Wh Aux NP X = Q
      Wh NP Aux X = E

Would these rules be selected by the evaluation metric over all other possibilities? The answer appears to be in the negative, since at least one alternative analysis is simpler than (12), namely, (13), which is

---

[6]Jackendoff (1972), Williams (1980), and Grimshaw (1977, 1979) give evidence for analyzing subject-auxiliary inversion and wh-fronting as optional. This analysis predicts that a matrix clause containing a wh-phrase can in principle have four possible realizations:

(i)	What has he done?	(+SAI, +wh-fronting)
(ii)	What a fool he has become!	(−SAI, +wh-fronting)
(iii)	He has done what?	(−SAI, −wh-fronting)
(iv)	Has he done what?	(+SAI, −wh-fronting)

All four possibilities are realized, (iii) and (iv) as echo questions.

[7]It is of course quite likely that when LAD is learning the grammar of matrix questions and exclamations, echo questions are not part of the database. If so, the simplest set of projection rules at this point would not in fact interpret (9b) and (10b), and the simplest grammar would not generate them. Although this may be true, it does not solve the problem of how the child knows that (9b) and (10b) are ill-formed. As soon as echo questions are analyzed, the simplest set of projection rules will interpret (9b) and (10b), so the problem simply reappears at a later point in time.

[8]These rules are based on the analysis given in Williams 1981a.

equally compatible with the positive evidence.

(13)   Wh X = Q / E

Thus a formal evaluation metric would never select the target grammar over grammar (13), and (13) predicts that (9c) and (10c) are well-formed.

So in this case, the theory of grammatical representation plus a formal evaluation metric is inadequate for the selection of the grammar. There is a plausible solution to the problem. The child hears only (9a) with an interrogative function, and (10a) with an exclamatory function. Suppose then that LAD incorporates a substantive evaluation metric which gives priority to a grammar with a one-to-one correspondence between form and function. The initial hypothesis will then be that (9a) is the only way of forming a wh question, and that (10a) is the only way of forming a wh exclamation. The rules in (12), those of the target grammar, will then be hypothesized rather than the formally simpler but incorrect (13).[9]

For the present example, there is never any need to revise the initial hypothesis. What of cases where form and function are not in one-to-one correspondence? Positive evidence will serve to trigger a change in hypothesis. Suppose LAD hears (14a) and hypothesizes the rule in (14b):

(14)   a.   Is he (ever) wrong?
       b.   Aux NP X = Q

When (15a) enters the data base – same form, different function – (14b) will simply be revised to (15b):

(15)   a.   Is he (ever) wrong!
       b.   Aux NP X = Q / E

So LAD will acquire the correct grammar when form and function do not correspond, as well as when they do.

What is the status of LAD's assumption that form and function correspond one-to-one? The theory of grammatical representation simply says that form and function *may* correspond, but there is no principled reason why they should. It certainly assigns no priority to correspondence over non-correspondence: quite the reverse, since correspondence is accidental, and non-correspondence is principled. It would obviously be unjustifiable to revise our theory of grammar to say that form and

---

[9]In fact, wh questions without subject-auxiliary inversion are generally produced before the adult forms, even though inversion is used in yes-no questions. This should probably be attributed to a complexity limitation on performance, rather than to an error of grammatical analysis.

function do correspond – this would incorrectly predict that pairs like (14a) and (15a) could not exist. So here we have evidence for a substantive evaluation metric.

3.4 Syntactic Categories

It is universally agreed by linguists that the syntactic categories of a language are defined in structural not semantic terms. Syntactic categorization is autonomous, since syntactic category membership is not reducible to meaning.

How are syntactic categories identified? The problem falls into two parts: LAD must group words and phrases together into classes, and must assign the appropriate labels to those classes. UG simplifies the task considerably: if LAD can analyze words correctly, X' theory will project the categorization of phrases from the lexical categorization (see Williams 1981b). But UG does not provide a universal structural definition for lexical categories.

Some developmental psycholinguists (e.g., Maratsos and Chalkley 1981) have argued that LAD can successfully determine category membership on the basis of purely distributional evidence. However, there seem to be a number of rather serious problems with this view, some of which are discussed in Pinker 1979.

Pinker points out that distributional analysis requires extremely large numbers of minimal pairs and that many errors will be made even if such pairs are provided: *Hottentots must fish* and *Hottentots eat fish* (from Pinker 1979) can only mislead LAD. Pinker also argues that the notion of "context," crucial for this account, is suspect: "Given n words in a sentence other than the item of interest, there are $2^n - 1$ different ways of defining 'context' for that item – it could be the word on the immediate right, the two words on the immediate left, the two flanking words, and so on" (p. 240).

This does not exhaust the difficulties: the distributional evidence for assigning words to categories rests on facts like cooccurrence with determiners, case-marking, agreement, complement type, word order, and so on. The particular factors, of course, vary from language to language. The difficulty is that many of these diagnostics depend on prior analysis of complex domains of grammar such as inflection. Many of these domains seem to be mastered quite late, well after the child starts to produce two- and three-word sentences that show evidence of grammatical categorization. Function words and morphemes are notoriously absent from children's "telegraphic" speech. Yet these are the very foundations of category learning, according to the distributional theory. Surely it is most unlikely that the child can use, and combine freely, words whose syntactic categories have not yet been ascertained.

Even if a purely distributional analysis could result in successful division of words into grammatical classes, it is not at all clear that the classes would be labeled appropriately. It is one thing to know that words fall into three major (open) categories, quite another to discover which class is the class of nouns, which the class of verbs, and so forth. What then prevents LAD from constructing a grammar like the one that generates (16)?

Note that (16) is entirely consistent with X′ theory. One might wonder whether it would matter if LAD did hypothesize (16). The answer is surely that it would be a disaster, given that universal constraints (such as Subjacency: Chomsky, 1977) make reference to categorial information. Given these problems, a purely distributional theory of category learning does not seem very promising.[10]

(16)

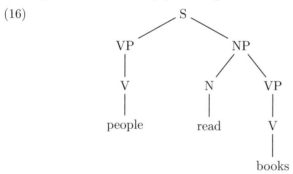

The issue can be resolved by a further hypothesis about the nature of LAD. There is plenty of evidence that at an early stage of linguistic development, children have ready command of semantico-cognitive categories like "object" and "action." Suppose then that LAD uses these categories as the basis for assigning syntactic categories to words. If a word is the name of an object, it is assigned the category N. If it

---

[10]It might seem that rather than trying to identify nouns and verbs and then projecting NP, VP, etc., from the lexical analysis, LAD could proceed by identifying NP, VP, and then deduce the lexical category from this. Would this make phrase structure learning easier? A phrase could perhaps be analyzed as an NP if it acted as a grammatical subject. But how would the subject be identified? Again, UG gives no universal definition of subject. What evidence there is suggests that grammatical relations are acquired via thematic relations – subject is initially identified with the agent, for example (see Pinker 1981). Apparently any theory of category acquisition must rely on some principle that relates grammatical category or function with nonsyntactic concepts.

describes an action, it is assigned the category V.[11] Thus certain cognitive categories have what I will call a Canonical Structural Realization (CSR): CSR (object) = N, CSR (action) = V. LAD employs a CSR principle: a word belongs to its CSR unless there is evidence to the contrary.

Of course the data will include many examples that cannot be analyzed this way, but these examples are likely to occur in relatively complex sentences that probably do not form part of the real data base at this point. In any event, should a sentence like *NP belongs to NP* occur, it will just have to be ignored.

LAD can construct phrase structure rules for NP and VP by drawing on example sentences whose lexical items can be assigned category labels by the CSR principle. In so doing, LAD will in effect be establishing a set of structural generalizations governing the distribution of N, V, and so on. These can be used as evidence for the analysis of any new categories (such as Det, Modal) for which no CSR is defined. The rules will also make it possible to assign category labels to words like *belong: belong* is a verb because it behaves like one with respect to the phrase structure rules. As for cases that would presumably be misanalyzed by the CSR principle, such as *destruction*, LAD will receive positive evidence about their categorization.[12]

---

[11] This solution is proposed in MacNamara 1982. Braine (1971) questions its validity. He taught his daughter the words *niss* and *seb*, with no syntactic context. *Niss* was said while pointing at an object, *seb* while performing an action. He reports that most of the time *niss* was used as a noun, *seb* as a verb, as one would predict. However, his daughter also produced *more seb*, and *bit more seb*, from which Braine concludes that she had a dual noun/verb categorization for *seb*. However, this argument depends on the assumption that the child's analysis of *more* is essentially the same as an adult's: it precedes nouns but not verbs. Given the frequency of utterances like *more tickle* in child language corpuses, it seems to me very likely that *more* is used indiscriminately before nouns and verbs and cannot be used as a test of categorization. However, I refer the reader to Braine's article for further details.

[12] If LAD misanalyzes a word, evidence will eventually emerge to show that the word belongs to another category. The difficulty is this: since the child would never receive evidence against the initial hypothesis, and since categorial ambiguity is not excluded by UG, why should the word not be treated as bicategorial? It appears that a mistake resulting from the CSR principle is irretrievable without negative evidence. If this were true, then there would of course be no cases of the crucial kind in any language. Any word that named an object would be a noun, whether or not it also belonged to another category. Note that the same issue arises in a distributional theory of category acquisition and that the problem seems similar to that posed by overregulation: how does the learner find out that *goed* does not exist? Baker (1979) suggests a solution based on frequency for the overregulation case, which could perhaps be extended to categorial learning. Some kind of uniqueness principle might provide an alternative account: assume that *go* + Past has only one

Universal grammar does not predict any particular relation between the meaning of a word and its syntactic category. LAD, however, uses a principle that expresses a dependency between syntactic and semantico-cognitive categories. What is the status of this dependency? The CSR principle could be viewed either as a matter of the theory of grammatical representation, or as a consequence of a substantive evaluation metric. For example, the theory of grammatical representation could be revised as follows:

(17) (i)   Syntax is autonomous.

      (ii) Certain perceptual/cognitive/semantic categories have corresponding syntactic categories in the unmarked case.

However, I think there is good reason to consider the CSR principle to be external to UG.

First, the joint effect of (i) and (ii) is odd: syntax is autonomous except when it isn't. Second, the CSR principle makes use of notions like "object" and "action," which are general cognitive notions and not specific to language. CSR itself thus expresses a relation between linguistic and nonlinguistic constructs. There is no independent evidence that UG makes reference to any of these concepts.

Note a trade-off between UG and LAD here. If the theory of LAD is enriched to subsume principles like that of CSR, which relate cognitive capacity and UG, the simple form of UG can be maintained together with the strongest version of the autonomy thesis. This in turn makes the potentially interesting prediction that systematic violations of autonomy (as opposed to accidental one-to-one correspondence) will be explicable in terms of the theory of acquisition.

3.5   Empirical Consequences of the Structure of LAD

The argument so far rests solely on the projection problem – without the suggested principles, the grammars of natural languages could not be learned. But clearly the proposal made here makes extremely strong predictions about the course of linguistic development. Although it is hard to disentangle the effects of cognitive development from the effects of these principles, the available evidence is at the very least consistent with the theory.

---

realization and that a word belongs to only one category unless there is direct and incontrovertible evidence to the contrary.

3.6 Consequences for the Course of Acquisition

The first words a child analyzes should be those that are categorized by the CSR principle: action verbs, names of objects, and so on. Some caution is in order here, because certain fixed expressions (*thank you*, *gimme*, and so on) may be learned but not analyzed syntactically at this point. So the prediction is that the words that are used productively, in accord with a set of phrase structure rules, will be of the appropriate type. It is quite well established that this is the case. (See the discussion in Brown, 1957, 1973, for a summary of some relevant material.) Brown (1957) and Katz, Baker, and MacNamara (1974) report experiments that support the basic point that children assume a systematic correlation between syntactic categories and categories like "object" and "action." The evidence suggests that children use syntactic cues to help them identify word meanings. If, for example, a nonsense word is used in a verbal context, it is taken to describe an action. If it is used as a noun, it is taken to refer to an object. Here the converse of the CSR principle is apparently being invoked.

More generally, the first grammar LAD constructs is one in which there is a one-to-one mapping between syntactic category or form and semantic or cognitive function. From the linguistic output of a child producing two- or three-word sentences it will be extremely difficult to determine whether the child's grammar is stated in terms of syntactic or semantic rules and categories. A brief glance at almost any of the literature on early acquisition will testify to the accuracy of this prediction.

3.7 Consequences for Language

The preceding cases suggest that learnability is not simply a function of data + UG, but of Data + UG + cognitive capacity. This has further consequences. It might explain how a grammar can be learned. It may also be the explanation for some linguistic universals.

Clearly not all language universals follow from UG. For example, morphological irregularity is generally confined to common words. Surely UG does not include a statement to this effect. Rather, the mere fact that irregular forms must be learned case by case, and therefore must be heard to be learned, is an adequate explanation. If an extremely uncommon verb had an irregular past tense, it would not stay irregular for very long.

Suppose then that LAD uses the CSR principle. This would suggest an explanation for the fact that languages do in fact display non-autonomy in just this way. Names of objects are typically nouns, names of actions typically verbs (or deverbal nouns). It is not at all clear that UG could be revised to express these tendencies in any illuminating fashion, and the purely distributional theory of category acquisition certainly offers no explanation. The CSR principle does illuminate this correlation: learning (and therefore evidence) is required for the words where the correlation does not hold; no learning (and no evidence) is needed for words that conform to the principle.

A less obvious example arises in the theory of complement selection, already discussed. The evidence for the claim that subcategorization and selection are autonomous seems to be extremely strong; nevertheless there is a class of generalizations that cannot be explained by the theory. If subcategorization and selection are independent, all possible combinations of the two should be realized in lexical entries. Although we do find predicates that take only wh questions and predicates that take both wh and NP questions, we do not find the third possibility-predicates that take NP questions but not wh questions. A predicate of this third type could be described simply by the theory of complement selection, as one that subcategorized NP (but not S′), and selected Q. (The same point holds, mutatis mutandis, for predicates taking E and P.)

(18) Predicate [___NP] <___Q>

Thus in fact the set of predicates that take NP question complements is a (proper) subset of the predicates that take wh forms, but this is not explained by the theory.

A parallel problem is found with Null Complement Anaphora; why are there no predicates taking only null complements? Such predicates would be subcategorized for no complements, and would select P, Q, or E. In fact the Null Complement Anaphora predicates are again a (proper) subset of the predicates that take realized complements.

It is conceivable that these gaps in the lexicon are accidental, that predicates of the relevant type could exist, and might be discovered in, or introduced into, English at any time. However it is much more likely that the subset relation between these predicates represents a real generalization about the lexicon, which must have an explanation.

What then are the options? Abandoning the hypothesis that selection and subcategorization are autonomous might make it possible to solve these problems, but then there would be no explanation for the generalizations that motivate the autonomy thesis to begin with. If the autonomy hypothesis is correct, apparently the only option is to build into UG constraints that would rule out the impossible cases. For example one could add the statement: If a predicate selects P, Q, or E, then it must be subcategorized for S′. This is hardly illuminating. Why should there be relations of this kind between subcategorization and selection? Why should the subset relation expressed by this condition hold equally for P, Q, and E? After all, the stipulation could just as well mention P and Q only, or Q and E only. Similarly, why S′? Why shouldn't the requirement be that a predicate that selects P, Q, or E must be subcategorized for AP, or NP?

It appears then that there is no interesting way of capturing relations between selection and subcategorization within the formal model of grammar. What I want to suggest is that the explanation for the subset relation may not be a matter of grammar at all; that it is not a problem for which linguistic theory should provide a solution. It can instead be viewed as a consequence of learning: a language that did not demonstrate the subset relation would be *representable*, but not *learnable*.

The notion of canonical structural realization can illuminate this problem. It seems extremely plausible that expressions of the semantic types P, Q, and E also have CSRs and that the correct CSR for all three is S′. Suppose then that there is a principle to this effect: If a predicate selects a semantic type, it is subcategorized for the CSR of that type. I will call this the Context Principle. This principle can be viewed as an absolute requirement, or it can be interpreted as determining the unmarked case. The marked case would be unlearnable, because it would require negative evidence, so either formulation correctly predicts that the subset relation will hold absolutely.

The principle can be illustrated in the case where LAD receives evidence that a predicate takes NP questions but no evidence that it takes wh questions: (19) but not (20) is in the database.

(19)   I asked John the time.

(20)   I asked John what the time was.

Clearly LAD can posit [___NP] on the basis of (19). If *the time* is assigned the appropriate semantic representation, <___Q> can also be associated with *ask,* giving the lexical entry in (21). But LAD also knows that the CSR(Q) is S′. Thus, by the Context Principle, LAD adds [___S′] to the entry, giving (22).

(21)   *ask:* [___NP]   <___Q>

(22)   *ask:* [___NP/S′]   <___Q>

Of course if LAD's data had consisted of (20) and not (19), only [___S′] and <___Q> could be posited. There would be no evidence for [___NP], because NP is not the CSR of Q. Thus predicates that take wh questions and not NP questions should be possible, as of course they are.

The same result is obtained for Null Complement Anaphora. If LAD has the data in (23), (24) will be an impossible entry:

(23) John left. I know.

(24) *know*: [___]   <___P>

The Context Principle will force the addition of S′ to the entry, so on the basis of (23) the entry in (25) will be constructed:

(25) *know*: [___(S′)]   <___P>

Could the Context Principle be a principle of UG? I have discussed this issue in connection with category acquisition; similar reasoning would lead to the same conclusion here. The notion of CSR plays no discernible role in linguistic theory, but it does appear to play a significant role in acquisition. I have argued that in order to solve the logical problem of language acquisition we may have to enrich the theory of LAD in two ways. First, some of the choices that must be made between competing grammatical hypotheses depend on substantive evaluation metrics, like the one relating form and function. Second, acquisition draws on a conceptual characterization of the data, which feeds the theory of grammar. I have tried to show that this view has interesting consequences for the projection problem, for certain linguistic problems, and for language development. Principles like those proposed here may also form the basis for a theory of markedness in language.

If this line of reasoning is correct, solving the projection problem may depend not just on formulating the correct theory of universal grammar but also on a more general theory of the acquisition device.

Works Cited in Chapter 3

See References on page 129 for publication information on the following works cited in this chapter.

Baker 1979

Braine 1971

Brown 1957, 1973

Chomsky 1965, 1970b, 1975, 1977, 1986b

Chomsky and Lasnik 1977

Grimshaw 1977, 1979

Jackendoff 1972

Katz, Baker and MacNamara 1974

MacNamara 1982

Maratsos and Chalkley 1981

Peters 1972

Pinker 1979, 1981

Williams 1980, 1981a, 1981b

4

Datives, Feet and Lexicons

This paper pursues the predictability, and ultimately the learnability, of the dative double NP complement configuration, and the limitations on the predicates the configuration is found with. The paper grew out of a series of three presentations at the Boston University Language Development Conference, which addressed semantic restrictions on dative double NPs, prosodic restrictions on them, and ultimately the question of how learners might arrive at the right solution with no negative evidence. The hypothesis I propose extends previous work in defending the position that the ability of a verb to appear in both the NP-PP configuration and the NP-NP configuration is predictable: all verbs alternate if they are of the appropriate semantics and from the appropriate (native) sub-lexicon of English. Both requirements are necessary, but neither is sufficient, for alternation to be possible. However, I propose that speakers do not posit a "dative" rule with a stipulation restricting it to native words, as some important learning work has suggested (Mazurkewich and White 1984, Pinker 1989, Gropen et al. 1989). The task of a learner is to decide which sub-lexicon of English a given verb belongs to. All verbs affiliated with the native/Germanic lexicon admit both complementation possibilities, all verbs affiliated with the non-native/Romance lexicon admit only the prepositional realization of their Goal argument. The difference is one which holds between vocabularies and *not between lexical items within a vocabulary*.

4.1   The Semantic Properties of the Alternation

Since the publication of Baker 1979 the issue of how lexical generalizations are learned has been one of the major foci of research in language learnability. Baker argued that many rules, especially those which are stated over lexical entries, have exceptions. As a result they can be overgeneralized by a language learner and incorrectly extended to the exceptions. To correct overgeneralization seems to require the use of "negative evidence" – evidence that certain sentences are NOT in the language, hence the learnability problem. Overgeneralization is intimately connected to the issue of predictability. If it is possible to predict whether an item is subject to a given rule or not, then the learner does not need to determine a class of arbitrary exceptions. The learnability question shifts to how learners figure out the generalization to begin with, rather than how they find out about exceptions.

One of the important examples discussed by Baker was English datives, which have been central in the ensuing learnability debate. (Mazurkewich and White 1984, Pinker 1984, Bowerman 1987, Randall 1990, Gropen et al. 1989, Grimshaw 1989.) The dative alternation relates the use of the verb with a prepositional phrase argument in (1a) to the use with a noun phrase argument in (1b).

(1) a. They sent/returned the books *to their friends*.

   b. They sent/*returned *their friends* the books.

While verbs like *send* and *give* alternate between the two syntactic contexts, syntactically comparable verbs like *return* and *donate* do not, apparently acting as exceptions to the rule.

Braine (1971) and Baker (1979) drew the attention of linguists to an extremely important problem for the theory of language acquisition. The reasoning was essentially this: children must generalize in order to learn a language from a finite corpus, yet if they do generalize, they are in danger of *over*-generalizing, and generating ungrammatical sentences. Given that there is no negative evidence (see Brown and Hanlon (1970), Grimshaw and Pinker (1989) and Morgan and Travis (1989)), the theory predicts that learners will get stuck with over-general grammars, and have no way to get back on track.

The original conception of this problem was in terms of a transformational rule, or a rule relating subcategorization frames. Both predict over-general application, since any verb which takes an NP-to-NP complement should alternate, hence the learning problem.

(2) NP-1 [*to* NP-2] $\rightarrow$ NP-2 NP-1

(3) [__ NP-1 *to* NP-2] $\rightarrow$ [__ NP-2 NP-1]

The argument made in Grimshaw 1989 is that the generalization is not defined over configurational representations in the first place. Learners are not positing rules like (2) or (3), so they are not making generalizations about "verbs which take NP-*to*-NP." Instead, they are seeking the right way of expressing the arguments of predicates.

A learner who hears both *give NP-PP* and *give NP-NP* concludes that a possessional goal argument of the kind that *give* takes can be realized either as a PP or as an NP. Hence the learner makes a generalization about the grammatical behavior of such goal arguments in general. This is why the first NP in double NP structures like (1) is subject to a semantic constraint – it must be a *possessor* (Green 1974; Oehrle 1976; Goldsmith 1980; Stowell 1981; Mazurkewich and White 1984; Levin 1985; Pinker 1989).

Suppose, for instance, that the lexico-semantic representation of *give* looks like (4):

(4) *give*: x causes y to become in possession of z

A learner who observes that z can be realized as NP or as PP will generalize to other verbs with possessional goal arguments, but not to verbs which do not have such arguments, even if they do occur in the configuration NP-*to*-NP.

Grimshaw 1989 then argues that three major classes of verbs fail to participate in the alternation precisely because the critical phrase does *not* have the same semantic character as the critical argument of verbs like *give*. See Pesetsky 1995, Krifka 1999 for more recent argument along these lines. There are (at least) two ways in which an expression can be dissimilar to the goal argument of *give*. First, if the expression is not an argument in the first place, it will not appear in the relevant representation at all. It will be *consistent* with the lexical semantics of the predicate, of course, but it will not be *implicated* in it. In such a case, we would characterize the expression as an adjunct.[1] It will be impossible, then, for a speaker to make a generalization from the behavior of an argument of *give* to this expression – the two do not figure in the same representational system. There is a second way in which an expression can differ from the goal of *give*; it can be an argument of the predicate, but not the same kind of argument as the goal of *give*, hence it is not represented in the same way and there is no reason for a learner to make a generalization across the cases.

Why does the alternation fail with *fix* and *mend* in (5b), when it succeeds with *fix* and *mend* in (5a)?

(5) a. I'll fix/make a sandwich for the children;
         I'll fix/make the children a sandwich.

     b. I'll fix/make the radiator for the children;
         *I'll fix/mend the children the radiator.

---

[1] As an adjunct, it will normally be optional, so the prediction in this case is similar to that made by Randall (1987). Randall proposes that learners use a principle requiring that an optional element cannot precede an obligatory one, and that observed optionality allows learners to correct overgeneralized datives. The present proposal does not need to appeal to such a principle.

The reason is that the argument encoded in a PP in (5a) is a possessor. The argument encoded in a PP in (5b) is only a benefactive, and
presumably an adjunct. There is no reason for generalization from one
to the other.

Verbs of transfer of possession alternate. Transitive verbs expressing
manner of change of location fail to:

(6) a. I'll throw/pass/hand/push/shove/carry the book to the
         instructor.

     b. I'll throw/pass/hand/*push/*shove/*carry the instructor
         the book.

The directional argument (or perhaps adjunct) of *push, shove* etc. is not
a goal/possessor: note that it can be realized with other prepositions,
and with inanimate NPs as the complement to the preposition: *into the
closet* for example. Gropen et al. (1989) object to this analysis, on the
grounds that the *to* PP is optional with both *throw* and *pull*: *John threw
the box (to Mary)* and *John pulled the box (to Mary)*. Concluding that
the *to* phrase is an adjunct in both instances, they argue that neither
verb should alternate. The fact that *throw* does, and *pull* does not,
then invalidates the analysis of Grimshaw 1989, in their view. However,
I think this reasoning is not correct: optionality alone is not a reliable
indicator of adjunct status.

The verb *throw* differs from *give*, in that the *to* PP with *throw* can
be replaced with another directional preposition, as is the case with
push, shove etc.

(7) a. He threw the box towards/at/under the patient.

     b. He pushed the box towards/at/under the patient.

     c. *He gave the box towards/at/under the patient.

Hence we know that *throw* can take a directional argument or adjunct.
But this does not show that it always does. In fact the behavior of
throw is exactly that of a verb which can take *either* type of argument
structure: it can take either a directional, like *push, shove* etc., or a pos-
sessive/goal. The goal variant occurs with NP-NP complements. This
kind of reasoning is not circular. We are able to show that a verb like
throw occurs in the configurations accepted by *push* etc., and also in
the configurations accepted by *give*. This is an empirical claim. Krifka
(1999) reaches a similar conclusion, with a more precise implementation. He argues that verbs like *throw* express the manner of a causing
event, while verbs like *pull* express manner of both a causing event
and an event of movement. He analyzes the double NP configuration
as causative. Since the causative semantics has no movement event, no

verb requiring a specification of the manner of a movement event can ever appear in the double NP configuration.

A further non-alternating verb class involves the verbs of manner of speaking (Green 1974). The puzzle here is that *tell* does alternate, while *yell, murmur, shout* and *whisper* do not.

(8) a. I'll tell/*yell the answer to the class.

b. I'll tell/*yell the class the answer.

Again, however, we find that this difference is just one among many: the critical argument is optional with manner of speaking verbs, but obligatory with *tell*.

(9) a. *I told the answer.

b. I yelled/shouted the answer.

It alternates with other kinds of PPs for verbs like *yell*, but not for *tell*.

(10) I yelled/*told the answer into the microphone.

Once again, there is no reason to believe that the lexico-semantic analysis of *yell* includes a component which matches the possessive goal-related component in the analysis of *give* in (4). Hence a learner who is working with this representation is in no danger of over-generalizing the alternation to the manner of speaking verbs.

In this view of lexical learning, the learner is not trying to learn conditions on a rule of dativization, whether lexical or syntactic. The learner must determine the correct lexico-semantic representation of each predicate, and must determine how each kind of semantic argument is realized in the language, in so far as this is not already decided at the universal level. A learner who knows which arguments are possessional goals, and that these goals can be realized as postverbal NPs, is in no danger of either under-generalizing or over-generalizing. To extend the pattern of argument-realization beyond this type would require a complication of the grammar, not a simplification, and there is no motivation for a learner to carry out the extension. This view in no way implicates the existence of a *rule* for double object datives of the kind proposed in Gropen et al. 1989 and Pinker 1989, which changes verb meaning from "cause Y to go to Z" to "cause Z to have Y." The existence of the semantic restriction to possessional goals follows from the nature of the semantic representations for verbs, and generalizations stated over them, such as those pertaining to argument realization.

4.2   The Prosodic Properties of the Verbs

Even within the semantic constraints outlined in the previous section, there is still variability among verbs with respect to the dative alternation: having a possessional goal argument is necessary, but not sufficient, for a verb to occur with both complement structures. (11)–(14) illustrate this. All of the cited verbs have possessional goal arguments, yet some allow this argument to be realized as a postverbal NP, and some do not. (Many marginal V-NP-NP examples are significantly better if the first NP is a pronoun than if it is a full phrase, so such examples do not definitively establish the properties of the predicate. I will cite only possessional goals which are full phrases.)

(11)   a.   She handed/delivered a letter *to the teacher*.
       b.   She handed/*delivered *the teacher* a letter.

(12)   a.   They sent/returned the books *to their friends*.
       b.   They sent/*returned *their friends* the books.

(13)   Some alternating verbs:
       accord advance allot allow assign award bring give grant hand leave lend loan mail offer owe pass pay promise send teach tell show

(14)   Some non-alternating verbs:
       address announce convey deliver dictate donate entrust explain present remit report return transfer

A key insight of earlier investigations is that the difference between verbs that do and do not allow the alternation is that the stems of alternating verbs are, with a few exceptions, monosyllables or bisyllables with a stressed initial syllable and unstressed second syllable. See for example Green 1974, Stowell 1981. Much learnability work (Mazurkewich and White 1984, Pinker 1989, Gropen et al. 1989) takes some form of this generalization to be basically correct and to provide a key insight into how the English dative might be correctly learned in the absence of negative evidence. This represents a significant change from the position of Baker 1979, which proposed conservative learning of a lexical stipulation which allows a verb to alternate.

I will argue here that the empirical generalization is fundamentally correct, and can be understood in terms of prosodic theory. However, I will also argue that the dative alternation is *not directly constrained by some kind of prosodic condition*.

The first significant point in favor of the prosodic proposal is that, as far as I can tell, there are no exceptions to the generalization that *all monosyllabic verbs alternate*, provided of course that they meet the semantic criterion of Section 4.1. This is a simple observation, but important, because it strongly supports the prosodic view of what governs the alternation over semantic or syntactic alternatives, or the view that the matter is arbitrary. None of these predict the uniform behavior of monosyllables (unless they themselves can be connected with monosyllabicity through some other theoretical machinery).

As for bisyllables, the claim is that they must have a stressed first syllable and unstressed second syllable in order to alternate: a strong–weak structure. There is, however, one systematic category of exceptions – a set of verbs including *allot, allow, assign, award*, and *advance* which all alternate despite having the wrong stress pattern: they are bisyllabic with stressed final syllables.

(15) a. They allotted/allowed/assigned *each passenger* one can of Coke.

   b. They awarded/advanced *the recipient* a thousand dollars.

Despite their apparent idiosyncrasy, the behavior of these verbs can be understood in terms of the prosodic account, as we will see below.

Overall the phonological generalization fits the data remarkably well; too well, it seems, to support the claim that alternation is not phonologically regular. We really do not want to predict that *return* and *donate* are as much candidates for alternation as *promise* and *offer*.

Why should the ability of a verb to appear with two different complement configurations depend on its stress? Ultimately, the answer I will propose is that it doesn't, not directly. But it does depend on what kind of morpheme the verb is, and this is related to its prosodic analysis into *feet*. The alternating verbs have a particular status in this theory – they are the ones whose stems form single feet. In other words, the phonological category involved in the dative alternation is one which UG defines independently.

The key to the generalization lies in the theory of prosodic constituents, which defines such units as the *syllable*, and larger prosodic units called *feet* and *prosodic words*. (Selkirk 1980a, 1980b, Nespor and Vogel 1982, 1986. See Kager 1995 for a useful review.) Every prosodic constituent has a head, or most prominent member. A prosodic word contains one prominent foot, its head, written as F'. A foot must contain one stressed syllable, its head, for which I use the symbol S'. It may in addition contain one non-head (i.e. unstressed) syllable, or S. For English the head (i.e. the strongest or most prominent member of the foot) must be initial in the foot. So a foot can be constructed of a single stressed syllable (16a), or a sequence of two syllables, the first stressed, the second unstressed (16b).

(16) a.

   b.

An unstressed syllable can never count as a foot, nor can a sequence of syllables with more than one stressed element. For English no sequence of syllables with any non-initial syllable stressed is ever a foot.

Expletive infixation provides additional evidence for the theory of prosodic constituents:

(17) a.

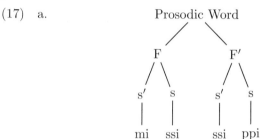

   b.

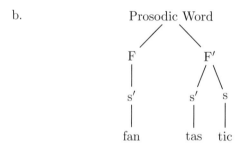

An expletive can be inserted only between feet (McCarthy 1982). It is possible to insert *fuckin'* between the feet in (17a) *missi-fuckin'-ssippi* and (17b) *fan-fuckin'-tastic*. Other placements lead to ill-formedness:

(18) a. *mi-fuckin'-ssissippi
      b. *mississi-fuckin'-ppi
      c. *fanta-fuckin'-stic

The theory of prosodic structure applies to the problem of analyzing (13) and (14) in this way: monosyllabic stems and disyllabic stems with initial stress and final unstressed syllables all form single feet.

(19) a. monosyllables: Prosodic Word

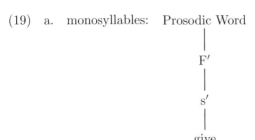

b. bisyllables: Prosodic Word

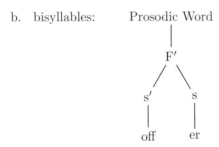

(20)

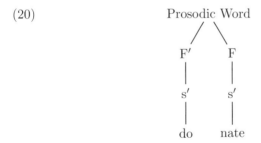

(21)

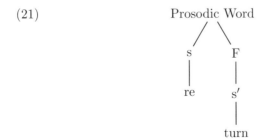

Bisyllables with a stressed final syllable can never have both syllables grouped into a single foot, and must be analyzed as in (20), with two feet, or as in (21), with one foot preceded by an unstressed syllable.

The principle governing alternation is summarized in (22). A verb admits the NP-NP complement structure if its stem is a prosodic word which in turn is a foot. (See McCarthy and Prince 1990, 1995, 1999 and references therein for effects of prosodic constituents in morphology, and the reduction of templatic requirements to constraint satisfaction.)

(22)   stem = prosodic word = foot

There is a class of unstressed prefixes which are systematically ignored in the computation of the prosodic weight of a stem (see Downing 1998). We can build on this to explain the behavior of the class of apparent exceptions to the generalization exemplified in (15) above: verbs with initial [ə] pattern with the single foot cases rather than the multiple foot cases. The verb *bequeath* shares this property, perhaps for morphological reasons (See also Section 4.3 and footnote 7.)

(23)   They allotted each passenger one can of Coke.

(24)

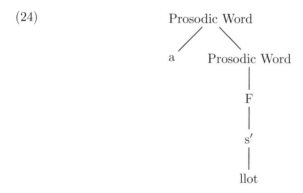

These verbs are treated as if they have a one-foot stem; as if the initial vowel is prosodically inert, or outside the prosodic word. These verbs distinguish the prosodic theory from the original phonological hypothesis, in which they are simply exceptional.

We can conclude that verb stems which consist of a prosodic word which dominates nothing more than a foot alternate. When the prosodic word dominates more than a foot, the verb cannot appear in the NP-NP complement configuration. Here, then, I differ from the conclusions of Zwicky and Pullum (1986). They argue that there is no phonological generalization governing the dative alternation, on the grounds that there are both alternating and non-alternating monosyllables and bisyllables with initial and final stress. Their assumption, however, is that satisfaction of the phonological requirement for alternation is both necessary and sufficient for alternation: in fact it is necessary but not sufficient. The semantic requirement of having a possessional goal must also be satisfied for a verb to alternate. They cite (based on Green 1974) four non-alternating anglo-Saxon monosyllables. Two, *lift* and *raise*, take directional PPs, not possessional goals (cf. the analysis of (6)) The others, *lisp* and *yell*, are manner of speaking verbs, which also lack possessional goals, as we saw in Section 4.1.[2]

The proposal that the constraint on the dative alternation is foot-based goes beyond the alternatives in a number of respects. It connects the option of alternation with prosodic theory and thus explains why the observed patterns take the form they do: foot versus more-than-foot. It shows that the learner does not have to look for all logically possible phonological restrictions on words: the generalization could not be that stems alternate if they are monosyllabic or have two syllables of which the second is stressed, or if they are disyllabic or trisyllabic with penultimate stress, or if they have an initial velar. These are not uniformly characterized in prosodic theory, while the class of feet is. Finally, the foot proposal accommodates the otherwise exceptional status of the stems with an unstressed initial vowel, reducing this to the known characteristics of stems of this form. The prosodic theory suggests a partial explanation for the fact that children notice the generalization – they have to analyze words into feet quite independently of the complement structures of various predicates.

Despite its descriptive merits, the foot-based proposal ultimately falls short as an explanation for learnability. The logic of the attempted explanation is this: we find an apparently arbitrary distinction in grammar, we show that it is not arbitrary because it correlates with something else, hopefully some observable property, and we conclude that the learner observes the correlating property. We could, for example, hypothesize that lexical rules, or the occurrence of particular complement structures, can be subject to phonological restrictions, but only when the restrictions concern prosodic categories – foot, syllable etc. This will at least reduce the learning problem to deciding that a restriction exists, and deciding which prosodic phenomenon is involved (instead of searching through all possible combinations of phonological

---

[2]Zwicky and Pullum (1986) also point to the fact that *promise* alternates while *donate* does not as evidence against a phonological generalization. However, while both have initial main stress, the two verbs differ in the status of their second syllable. Only *promise* has a reduced, i.e. weak, second syllable, and constitutes a single foot.

properties). However it does not tell us how learners decide that a restriction exists to begin with. For this, we still need to assume some kind of conservative learning.

The problem is that what we have found is a correlation, not an explanation. The fact that foot/more-than-foot correlates with complement structure possibilities *does not mean that alternation depends on prosodic structure.* We have no theory of the relationship between prosodic structure and complementation which even allows us to state this regularity. And it follows that the learner has no theory of the relationship, and cannot use the prosodic structure to learn the alternation patterns.

So we have not made much progress on the learnability issue, merely uncovered an improved formulation of a regularity in English grammar. We don't understand why the connection between prosody and complement structure holds, and we don't understand why learners maintain it, rather than making the sweeping generalization that leads to an apparently regular system in which all verbs occur in all syntactic contexts that are semantically appropriate.

Why on earth should prosody condition the dative alternation? The solution I propose in the next section is that it shouldn't and doesn't. *It is no more true that the prosody conditions the dative alternation than that the dative alternation conditions the prosody.* Instead, the prosody is related to vocabulary type, or sub-lexicon, and vocabulary type is in turn related to complementation possibilities.

4.3 English Speakers as Lexical Bilinguals

Let us accept, with some details still to be explored further, that English speakers have a completely general dative alternation pattern which meets the descriptions established in Sections 4.1 and 4.2: all verbs which have possessional Goals and constitute no more than a single foot, allow the Goal to be realized as an NP. It has been pointed out many times that the stress pattern of the alternating verbs is just one indication that they belong to the "native" vocabulary, while the others are latinate in origin. (See especially Green 1974, Oehrle 1976, Stowell 1981). The native vocabulary differs in several additional respects from the latinate lexicon, as documented in Chomsky and Halle 1968, Aronoff 1976 (see below for some examples).

An observer who knows the solution to the puzzle is able to predict which verbs alternate: in this sense the existence of both structures for some verbs is "predictable." This does not entail that a learner who does not know the solution can predict that some verbs will lack one of the structure, and which ones. And we have no reason to think that the learner already knows the solution. So the insight that a native/non-native distinction lies behind the alternation patterns does not of itself resolve the learnability issue.

Recent attempts to connect the native status of the verbs with their alternation patterns posit a rule, together with conditions on that rule which limit it to native stems. These proposals are quite different, but they share the important core: there is a rule and the rule applies to a particular set of verbs.

Mazurkewich and White (1984) (see also Pinker 1984) suggest that learners initially formulate a rule which is more general than the adult's; lacking both the restriction to possessors, and any connection to the native/non-native distinction. Later, when they have "observed that this distinction is relevant for verbs," they check the verbs which occur in the NP-NP configuration, determine that they are native, and add the restriction to the rule.

Gropen et al. 1989 and Pinker 1989 argue that the dative alternation is the result of application of a rule which changes argument structure, changing the meaning of a predicate from "cause Y to go to Z" to "cause Z to have Y."[3] This rule is a "broad-range" rule which predicts the nature of the relationship between two variants of a predicate, but not the existence of both. Narrow-range rules, defining semantic and morpho-phonological classes, predict which verbs actually alternate. If all the verbs that the child hears in the NP-NP configuration are native, the rule will be restricted to the native class of verbs.

Despite important differences among them, these proposals share three components. First, the learner in each case posits a rule (or set of rules) relating the two configurations of the dative alternation. Second, the learner in each case learns about the $+/-$ native distinction. Third, the learner uses the $+/-$ native distinction to demarcate the verbs, and thus limit the scope of application of the rule to native verbs only.

The proposal here denies the first and the third of these components. As noted in Section 4.1 it is not necessary to posit a rule to explain why the NP-NP configuration is limited to possessional Goals – this can be derived from "linking" principles, mapping semantic arguments into syntactic positions or roles. How then is the scope of application of the linking to be limited to native vocabulary? Furthermore, the hypoth-

---

[3]They argue that there is a meaning difference – relating to the "affectedness" of the possessor, between alternating and non-alternating verbs. This may well be an effect of structural realization, rather than a cause of it. See Gleitman et al. 1996 for an argument that structural position introduces apparent asymmetries in symmetrical predicates.

esis that a property like "constituting a single foot" or "being in the native vocabulary" can directly condition a rule makes the possibility of a restrictive theory of such rules extremely remote, for familiar and obvious reasons.

There is another perspective, in which the *give/donate* distinction is not one which holds within a single language, but one which holds between two different lexical systems. The idea is that learners are not deciding whether or not *give* and *donate* participate in some alternation. Instead, they are deciding which (sub-)lexicon each verb belongs to. Under this view, properties of the individual verbs do not determine their ability to appear in the NP-NP configuration. Properties of the verbs do determine their assignment to a (sub-)lexicon, and their (sub-)lexicon membership determines their complement possibilities, along with several other properties. Properties such as prosodic weight and morphology do not cause verbs to alternate, but they do correlate with alternation.

The lexicons that alternating and non-alternating verbs belong to differ in several respects. The discussion of Section 4.2 shows, under the new interpretation, that verbs with a stem which does not satisfy (22) fall into a different lexicon than verbs with one-foot prosody: the former belong to the non-native R(omance)-Lexicon, the latter to the native G(ermanic)-Lexicon. The existence of prosodic constraints on morphemes in sub-lexicons has been demonstrated previously. Itô and Mester (1995, 1999) review evidence showing that Japanese has four (sub-)lexicons: The native lexicon, called "Yamato"; the Sino-Japanese lexicon, containing words borrowed from Chinese, the Mimetic lexicon and the Foreign lexicon. The Sino-Japanese words are prosodically restricted to monosyllables: each root is a single S. Roots in the Mimetic lexicon must be single feet.

Correlating with the prosodic division among English roots are other phonological properties. For example the process of velar softening, as in *critic, criticize, criticism* is limited to the vocabulary of the R-lexicon. The lexicons differ morpho-syntactically as well. G-lexicon verbs can have irregular past forms; *give, gave*. According to Pinker and Prince 1988: 114, there are 180 irregular past tense morphemes, 90% of them monosyllabic and the rest "composed of a monosyllable combined with an unstressed and essentially meaningless prefix." R-Lexicon verbs are regular. Particular prefixes and suffixes are associated with the R-lexicon: *in-*; *im-*; *-ity* etc.; or the G-lexicon: comparative *-er*, for example. Verbs (with causative meanings) which nominalize in the latinate affixes *-tion, -al, -ment*, have both transitive and intransitive derived nominals. Others occur sporadically and intransitively (Smith 1972).

Verbs with latinate nominalizations have "complex event" interpretations and preserve the argument structure of the verb (Grimshaw 1990).

It is important to emphasize that I am not claiming that learners have access to information about which words originated in Old English and which came from French (or elsewhere). The hypothesis is rather that they do divide words into (at least) two classes based on their linguistic properties, and for historical reasons, these linguistic properties correlate with the historical source of the word. There are many cases in which words which are historically from one source are analyzed by speakers as part of the other system, *promise* and *offer* among them (Green 1974).

The sub-lexicon hypothesis affects the learnability picture in a radical way. There *are no principles operative within a grammar that decide whether an alternation is possible or not*. Learners do not compare *give* and *donate* as if they were two words of the same language, just as we do not compare *donner* and *geven*, without taking into account the differences between French and Dutch. Rather the distinctions follow from principles operative between grammars. Learning is a matter of distinguishing the G-lexicon from the R-lexicon, not distinguishing one word from another within a single lexicon.

Why do G-lexicon verbs alternate? The hypothesis is this: the semantics of a verb with a theme and a possessor/Goal argument are compatible with at least two realizations of the arguments. Whether both realizations occur within a given language depends on the grammar of the language, and on what complementation possibilities it makes available. I assume that every grammar allows for the possibility of an NP complement combining with a PP complement, where the P marks possessional Goals. However, not every grammar allows for the possibility of two NP complements. For present purposes we can remain agnostic on the mechanisms underlying such complementation options: morphological or abstract case-marking, theta-marking, subcategorization, or principles of phrase structure (see Section 4.4 for discussion).

Verbs in the G-lexicon alternate because the morphosyntax associated with the G-lexicon supports double object complementation. Hence *give* and *hand*, which have possessional Goal arguments, and occur in a linguistic system where both realizations are grammatical, show the alternation. Verbs in the R-lexicon do not alternate because the morphosyntax of the R-lexicon supports only single object complementation. Hence *donate* and *deliver*, even though they too have possessional Goal arguments, cannot take NP-NP complement structures, i.e. cannot "alternate," because the complementation system will not allow it.

The *give/donate* contrast suggests that the R-lexicon has the Romance grammatical system which licenses only one complement NP, while the G-lexicon has the Germanic grammatical system which licenses two. The verb *donate* fails to alternate because it belongs to a lexicon with the wrong complement-taking possibilities. The following examples from Danish, Dutch, German and Icelandic illustrate the grammaticality of NP-NP complement configurations for verbs with the familar semantics:[4]

(25)   Han sendte sin sekretær blomster
        He   sent   his secretary flowers
        (Danish: Herslund 1986: 125)

(26)   ...dat Jan   zijn vader een boek geeft
        ...that John his father a book   gives
        (Dutch: Neeleman and Weerman 1999: 45)

(27) a. ... daß der Hans der Maria   das Buch gibt
        ... that the Hans the Maria (DAT) the book gives

    b. ... daß der Hans das Buch der Maria   gibt
       ... that the Hans the book the Maria (DAT) gives
       (German: den Dikken 1995: 135)

(28) a. Jón gaf konunginum   ambáttina
        John gave the-king(DAT) the-maidservant

    b. Jón gaf ambáttina   konunginum
       John gave the-maidservant the-king(DAT)
       (Icelandic: den Dikken 1995: 135)

The question of exactly which verbs occur in the two structures has not been a focus of research in Germanic languages other than English; I infer that puzzles of the *give/donate* variety have not been discovered there.

In contrast to the Germanic examples, French disallows the NP-NP configuration:

(29)   *Jean a donné   Marie un livre
        John has given Mary a book
        (French: Kayne 1984: 193)

The same is true in Spanish (see Demonte 1995).

---

[4]Note that both German and Icelandic allow both orders for the NP-NP complement structure. See den Dikken 1995 for discussion.

The broad finding, then, is that Germanic verbs appear with two NP complements, while Romance verbs do not. But this is not due to properties of the individual verbs, it is due to properties of the language that they are part of, or at least its lexicon. If the argument I'm making here is correct, the same is true for alternating and non-alternating datives within English. We cannot compare *give* and *donate* as if they were two words of the same language.

This relates the within-language difference between alternating and non-alternating verbs to the between-language difference between strict NP-PP complement systems, and systems which admit also NP-NP complement structures. Differences between verbs in a given language must reflect UG options displayed in other languages.

If language learners can posit and maintain more than one lexicon, there is no particular reason why they should be limited to two, and indeed Itô and Mester's work cited previously argues that several sub-lexicons can be found in Japanese. This suggests a possible solution for a couple of empirical puzzles.

For some speakers (for example Green 1974, Randall 1987: 46–48, Gropen et al. 1989) verbs which describe transfer by modern technology (Green's "denominal instrumental communication verbs") seem to allow the NP dative regardless of prosodic structure: *satellite, telegraph, telephone*, for example.[5]

(30) a. We satellited/telgraphed/telephoned the information to the FBI.

      b. We satellited/telgraphed/telephoned the FBI the information.

Gropen et al. (1989: 208) cite several examples, of which the following violate the prosodic requirement on alternation:

(31) a. I satellited a message to him/I satellited him a message. (from Wasow 1981)

      b. Please xerox me a copy.

      c. She bitnetted me the latest version.

Verbs such as these may well be isolated by speakers from other sub-lexicons of the language, and assigned to a sub-lexicon which is not circumscribed by the prosodic requirement and which has a grammar which allows the double NP complement structure. For such speakers, these verbs will "alternate" freely. While some speakers are less happy than others with examples of this kind – note that Gropen

---

[5]The fact that these verbs are denominal may be important here.

et al. cite them with pronominal goal arguments, giving maximal well-formedness – the literature contains too many instances to ignore. This is problematic for a purely prosodic account, it makes sense under the lexical multi-lingualism perspective.

A handful of other verbs which do not satisfy the prosodic description, including *allocate, guarantee* and *bequeath* sound marginally acceptable (as always, best with a pronoun as the indirect object, less good with a full NP).[6]

(32) a. They allocated/guaranteed us/each student/?the students a thousand dollars for travel.

b. She bequeathed them/her family a thousand dollars.

The literature on the topic has noted that verbs of future possession seem to have distinctive properties (Green 1974, Gropen et al. 1989). This may be attributable to the principles governing the realization of a future possessional goal, but their status with respect to alternation needs to be explored.[7]

In this model all semantic candidates for alternation which are in the G-lexicon should alternate. None in the R-lexicon should alternate. Provided that there is no means available to introduce irregularity, i.e. provided that no lexicon-internal stipulation is possible, there should be complete regularity and predictability within each lexicon. (From the point of view of linguistic theory, this suggests there is simply no way to stipulate the difference between an alternating and a non-alternating verb within a sub-lexicon. If such a means existed, there should be irregularity within the G-lexicon, with some verbs arbitrarily unable to participate in one of the structures.) Is the prediction correct? Testing it obviously requires accurate understanding of the semantic requirement for realization of a Goal as an NP. It also requires accurate analysis of the vocabulary affiliation of verbs, which is not a straightforward matter. For example, Zwicky and Pullum cite the verbs *prove* and *voice*

---

[6]While *guarantee* occurs comfortably in the NP-NP configuration, in the NP-PP configuration it has an additional requirement: *They guaranteed a large stipend to him* seems ungrammatical to me. To make it grammatical the object of the preposition must be made heavy: *They guaranteed a large stipend to every student who applied.* This effect is unexplained.

[7]In addition, *bequeath* contains the *be-* prefix. There are a number of prefixes which introduce strong, i.e. irregular verbs, which do not satisfy the Germanic foot template: *a-, be-, for-, under-* and *with-* (Pinker and Prince 1988: n. 19). This suggests that these prefixes are taken as indicating Germanic lexicon status, regardless of prosody, predicting that *bequeath* should be analyzed as Germanic, and hence alternate. (It is possible that it is the prefix itself, rather than the prosody of the verb as a whole, which is responsible for the verbs with [ə] analyzed in Section 4.2.)

as non-Anglo-Saxon and non-alternating. Should they participate in both structures, according to the present hypothesis? If speakers assign them to the G-lexicon, which presumably they do, and if the relevant argument is a possessional Goal, then the NP-NP structure should be compatible with them. The issue turns, then, on whether *to the committee* in *She proved the point to the committee,* and in *She voiced her concerns to the committee*, is, or can be, a possessional Goal. Further analyses along the key dimensions will clarify just how accurate the predictions are.

4.4   Learning and Linguistic Representation

This model raises a couple of important questions about linguistic representation. It assumes that the first NP in an NP-NP configuration and the object of the preposition in a NP-PP configuration are both consistent with the semantics of predicates with possessional Goals, and that the syntax of English supports both structures. However, the sub-lexicon determines which among the semantically and syntactically legitimate configurations its members can in fact appear in, with the R-lexicon supporting the Romance complement system, and the G-lexicon participating in the more liberal Germanic complement system. How does this happen?

Research on what distinguishes Germanic and Romance languages with respect to the dative alternation has generally focused on case-marking, e.g. Kayne 1984, den Dikken 1995. Kayne (1984) proposed that the Goal argument in an NP-NP structure is accompanied by a null preposition. (See Pesetsky 1995 for a related analysis.) In English this preposition inherits an objective case from the verb, and transmits it to the first NP complement. Assignment of objective case by a P is possible only in a language where prepositions generally assign objective (rather than inherent) case. Since French is not such a language, a null P cannot assign case to the first NP, and a Goal argument with no overt preposition will fail to be case-marked.

In Larson 1988 this idea is developed in the context of a complex VP structure. Dative shift, in Larson's perspective is the raising of a goal into a specifier of VP position, from a VP internal position. The theme receives (inherent) objective case from the lower V position (technically a reanalyzed V′), and the goal receives (structural) objective case from the raised V, in the Specifier of VP (Larson 1988: 359–361). Since structural case can be absorbed, but inherent case cannot, the preposition *to* which assigns case in the NP-PP configuration can undergo absorption, resulting in the NP-NP structure. If prepositions in the Romance languages assign only inherent case, as proposed in Kayne 1981, these languages will not have NP-NP structures, since absorption will not be possible. Such an account connects the Romance versus Germanic contrast to other important differences between their grammars (Larson 1988: 379–380).

A completely different possibility is that Romance verbs can govern/assign case to their complements, but not to the specifiers of their complements. If the structure of an NP-NP dative is like Larson's (1988), where the Goal is the specifier of the complement to *send* in *Mary sent a letter*, Romance verbs could never allow the NP-NP structures. Moreover, if prepositions share this property with verbs, both the impossibility of exceptional case-marking and the absence of complementizers like *for* will also follow. (See Kayne 1981 for an argument that the two are correlated.) Of course Germanic verbs must differ in accessing the specifiers of their complements.

Yet another interpretation, which avoids associating case-marking with a sub-lexicon directly, is that the syntax of the extended projection may depend on the lexical affiliation of its head. A G-lexicon head occurs in a complex VP structure, for instance of the kind proposed in Larson 1988. An R-lexicon head occurs only in a simplex VP structure, with just one VP projection. Under a slightly different scenario, the syntax of functional projections may depend on the lexical affiliation of their extended head, as defined in Chapter 1. If a functional head responsible for licensing an NP in its specifier can be erected over a native-headed lexical projection, but not over a latinate-headed lexical projection, the language internal pattern would follow.

What do these hypotheses imply for speakers of English? Under the accounts focusing on prepositions, speakers must have the structural case assigning P with Germanic verbs, and only the inherent case assigning P with Romance verbs. To put it another way, Germanic verbs will allow absorption of the prepositions *to/for*, while Romance verbs will not. This seems to shift the burden of determining case marking from the case assignment properties of prepositions themselves to the properties of verbs in determining absorption possibilities. Under the view that Germanic verbs access the specifier of their complement, as well as the complement itself, speakers must attribute the more liberal definition of the relationship between a Germanic verb and its complement, and the less liberal definition for a Romance verb. If the extended projection of an R-verb is different from that of a G-verb, the theory of extended projection in Chapter 1 needs to be modified, perhaps requiring a match in a G/R feature for some heads above the lexical head in the extended projection.

The multi-lexicon hypothesis explains why the *give/donate* contrast has been found to correlate with a number of other properties, some listed above, *while not reducing to any of them*. The correlating properties are those of the individual lexicons and associated grammatical properties, not properties of verbs which cause them to alternate. There are no principles operative within a grammar to decide which among the verbs of the right semantics will alternate and which will not. Hence there are no arbitrary gaps to be learned, and no negative evidence is needed to learn them.

Where does this leave the learning issue? At first glance, it appears to solve it. We know that people can learn multiple languages so presumably they can learn multiple lexicons. But how exactly do they do it? Unlike the case of bilingual language exposure, the lexical items of English all appear in the same core syntactic configurations, with the same functional heads and so forth. A learner in a bilingual situation hears French words in French sentences with French syntax, and English words in English sentences with English syntax, but the learner of English is not so lucky. The linguistic context does not naturally divide verbs into sub-lexicons.

And there is a more important problem – *why* do language learners preserve distinct lexicons with different properties, instead of simply merging them all into one coherent whole? Of course, this issue arises with equal force in theories which hold that a rule is restricted to +/−native, such as the Gropen et al. 1989 and Mazurkewitch and White 1984 proposals. These theories require that a learner separate words into native and non-native, *and* that they tag a rule as restricted to the native class.

What must be true is that maintaining multiple vocabularies is low-cost or no-cost for learners, since it's certainly a low- or no-benefit proposition. Presumably, high sensitivity to semantic, prosodic and morphological characteristics of words makes it so easy for learners to separate vocabularies that they might as well do it, even if it is not obviously useful. There is also a clear difference in frequency, time of exposure and register between the two vocabularies (see Gropen et al. 1989 for discussion). These may facilitate preservation of the distinction.

A final question concerns the nature of the organization of the English lexicon. Does it bifurcate into two disjoint sets of morphemes, or are the sets of morphemes partially overlapping, or organized into a core-periphery structure as Itô and Mester (1995, 1999) argue for Japanese? They take the position that "the more nativized an item, the more it is exempt from lexical constraints." (1995: 824). This is not simple to interpret as it applies to English dative verbs. The R-verbs do not have to satisfy the condition on prosodic words (22), the G-verbs do. On the other hand, the G-verbs have more complementation options than the R-verbs and in this respect the R-verbs seem more constrained.

In sum, the learnability problem for the dative alternation is not fully resolved by the hypothesis that the grammar of the G-lexicon admits two complement structures and the grammar of the R-lexicon admits only one. However, the proposal sheds new light on the relationship between the prosody of a verb and its ability to alternate, and revises our conception of the learning issues surrounding the dative alternation.

Works Cited in Chapter 4

See References on page 129 for publication information on the following works cited in this chapter.

Aronoff 1976
Baker 1979
Bowerman 1987
Braine 1971
Brown and Hanlon 1970
Chomsky and Halle 1968
Demonte 1995
den Dikken 1995
Downing 1998
Gleitman, Gleitman, Miller and
  Os-Trin 1996
Goldsmith 1980
Green 1974
Grimshaw 1989, 1990
Grimshaw and Pinker 1989
Gropen, Pinker, Hollander,
  Goldberg and Wilson 1989
Herslund 1986
Itô and Mester 1995, 1999
Kager 1995
Kayne 1981, 1984

Krifka 1999
Larson 1988
Levin 1985
Mazurkewich and White 1984
McCarthy 1982
McCarthy and Prince 1990, 1995,
  1999
Morgan and Travis 1989
Neeleman and Weerman 1999
Nespor and Vogel 1982, 1986
Oehrle 1976
Pesetsky 1995
Pinker 1984, 1989
Pinker and Prince 1988
Randall 1987, 1990
Selkirk 1980a, 1980b
Smith 1972
Stowell 1981
Wasow 1981
Zwicky and Pullum 1986

References

Abney, S. 1987. The English Noun Phrase in its Sentential Aspect. Doctoral dissertation, MIT.

Ackema, P. 2001. Colliding complementizers in Dutch: Another Syntactic OCP Effect. *Linguistic Inquiry* 32:717–726.

Anderson, M. 1979. Noun Phrase Structure. Doctoral dissertation. University of Connecticut.

Aronoff, M. 1976. *Word Formation in Generative Grammar*. MIT Press.

Austin, P. and J. Bresnan. 1996. Non-configurationality in Australian Aboriginal Languages. *Natural Language and Linguistic Theory* 14:215–268.

Baker, C. L. 1968. Indirect Questions in English. Doctoral dissertation. University of Illinois.

Baker, C. L. 1979. Syntactic Theory and the Projection Problem. *Linguistic Inquiry* 10:533–581.

Baker, M. 1988. *Incorporation: A Theory of Grammatical Function Changing*. Chicago: University of Chicago Press.

Baker, M. and K. Hale. 1990. Relativized Minimality and Pronoun Incorporation. *Linguistic Inquiry* 21:289–297.

Baker, C. L. and J. J. McCarthy eds. 1981. *The Logical Problem of Language Acquisition*. MIT Press.

Baltin, M. 1989. Heads and Projections. In M. Baltin and A. Kroch eds. *Alternative Conceptions of Phrase Structure*, 1–16. Chicago: Chicago University Press.

Baltin, M. 1995. Floating Quantifiers, PRO and Predication. *Linguistic Inquiry* 26:199–248.

Bayer, J. 1984. Comp in Bavarian Syntax. *The Linguistic Review* 3:209–274.

Bayer, J. 1996. *Directionality and Logical Form: On the Scope of Focusing Particles and wh-in-situ*. Dordrecht: Kluwer.

Bayer, J. and A. Grosu. 2000. Feature Checking meets the criterion approach: three ways of saying *only* in Romance and Germanic. In V. Motapanyane ed. *Comparative studies in Romanian syntax*, 49–81. Amsterdam; New York: Elsevier.

Beerman, D. 1990. Semantic and Syntactic Constraints on German Determiner Movement within the Prepositional Phrase. MA thesis, University of Texas at El Paso.

Belletti, A. 2001. Agreement Projections. In M. Baltin and C. Collins eds. *The Handbook of Contemporary Syntactic Theory*, 483–510. Malden, Mass.: Blackwell.

Bennis, H. and L. Haegeman. 1984. On the Status of Agreement and Relative Clauses in West-Flemish. In W. de Geest and Y. Putsey eds. *Sentential Complementation*, 33–53. Dordrecht: Foris.

Bhatt, R. and J. Yoon. 1992. On the Composition of COMP and Parameters of V2. *Proceedings of the Tenth West Coast Conference on Formal Linguistics*, 41–53.

Bittner, M. and K. Hale. 1996. The Structural Determination of Case and Agreement. *Linguistic Inquiry* 27:1–68.

Bobaljik, J. and D. Jonas. 1996. Subject Positions and the Roles of TP. *Linguistic Inquiry* 27:195–236.

Borsley, R. and J. Kornfilt. 2000. Mixed Extended Projections. In R. Borsley ed. *The Nature and Function of Syntactic Categories*, 101–131. San Diego: Academic Press.

Bowerman, M. 1987. The "No Negative Evidence" Problem: How Do Children Avoid Constructing an Overly General Grammar? In J. Hawkins ed. *Explaining Language Universals*, 73–101. Oxford; New York: Blackwell.

Braine, M. 1971. On Two Models of the Internalization of Grammars. In D. Slobin ed. *The Ontogenesis of Grammar; A Theoretical Symposium*, 153–186. New York: Academic Press.

Brame, M. 1981. The General Theory of Binding and Fusion. *Linguistic Analysis* 7:277–325.

Brame, M. 1982. The Head-Selector Theory of Lexical Specifications and the Nonexistence of Coarse Categories. *Linguistic Analysis* 10:321–325.

Bresnan, J. and S. Mchombo. 1987. Topic, Pronoun, and Agreement in Chichewa. *Language* 63:741–782.

Brown, R. 1957. Linguistic Determinism and the Part of Speech. *Journal of Abnormal and Social Psychology* 55:1–5.

Brown, R. 1973. *A First Language: The Early Stages*. Harvard University Press.

Brown, R. and C. Hanlon. 1970. Derivational Complexity and Order of Acquisition in Child Speech. In J. Hayes ed. *Cognition and the Development of Language*, 155–207. New York: Wiley.

Büring, D. and K. Hartmann. 2001. The Syntax and Semantics of Focus-Sensitive Particles in German. *Natural Language and Linguistic Theory* 19:229–281.

Cardinaletti, A. and G. Giusti. 2001. "Semi-lexical" motion verbs in Romance and Germanic. In Norbert Corver and Henk van Riemsdijk eds. *Semi-lexical categories*, 371–414. Mouton de Gruyter.

Cheng, L. 1991. On the Typology of Wh-Questions, Doctoral Dissertation, MIT.

Cheng, L. 1995. On dou-quantification. *Journal of East Asian Linguistics* 4:197–234.

Choi, S. and M. Bowerman. 1991. Learning to Express Motion Events in English and Korea. *Cognition* 41:83–121.

Chomsky, N. 1957. *Syntactic Structures*. The Hague: Mouton.

Chomsky, N. 1965. *Aspects of the Theory of Syntax*. MIT Press.

Chomsky, N. 1970a. Remarks on Nominalization. In R. Jacobs and P. Rosenbaum eds. *Readings in English Transformational Grammar*, 184–221. Waltham, Mass.: Ginn and Co.

Chomsky, N. 1970b. *Current Issues in Linguistic Theory*. The Hague: Mouton.

Chomsky, N. 1975. Questions of Form and Interpretation. *Linguistic Analysis* 1:75–109.

Chomsky, N. 1977. On wh-movement. In P. Culicover, T. Wasow and A. Akmajian eds. *Formal Syntax*, 71–132. New York: Academic Press.

Chomsky, N. 1986a. *Barriers*. MIT Press.

Chomsky, N. 1986b. *Knowledge of Language: its Nature, Origin and Use*. New York: Praeger.

Chomsky, N. 1993. A minimalist program for Linguistic Theory. In K. Hale and S. J. Keyser eds. *The View from Building 20: Essays in Linguistics in Honor of Sylvain Bromberger*, 1–52. MIT Press.

Chomsky, N. 1995. *The Minimalist Program*. MIT Press.

Chomsky, N. and M. Halle. 1968. *The Sound Pattern of English*. New York: Harper Row.

Chomsky, N. and H. Lasnik. 1977. Filters and control. *Linguistic Inquiry* 8:425–504.

Chung, S. 1990. VPs and Verb Movement in Chamorro. *Natural Language and Linguistic Theory* 8:559–619.

Chung, S. 1994. Wh-Agreement and "Referentiality" in Chamorro. *Linguistic Inquiry* 25:1–44.

Chung, S. and J. McCloskey. 1987. Government, Barriers, and Small Clauses in Modern Irish. *Linguistic Inquiry* 18:173–237.

Cinque, G. 1990. *Types of A' Dependencies*. MIT Press.

Cinque, G. 1994. On the Evidence for Partial N-Movement in the Romance DP. In G. Cinque, J. Koster, J.-Y. Pollock, L. Rizzi and R. Zanuttini eds. *Paths towards Universal Grammar: studies in honor of Richard S. Kayne*, 85–111. Washington, D.C.: Georgetown University Press.

Cinque, G. 1999. *Adverbs and Functional Heads*. New York; Oxford: Oxford University Press.

Cole, P., G. Hermon and L-M. Sung. 1993. Feature Percolation. *Journal of East Asian Linguistics* 2:91–118.

Corver, N. 1990. The Syntax of Left Branch Extractions. Doctoral dissertation, Tilburg University.

Corver, N. 1991. Evidence for DegP. *Proceedings of the North Eastern Linguistics Society Annual Meeting 21*, 33–47. GLSA. University of Massachusetts at Amherst.

Corver, N. 1997a. The Internal Syntax of the Dutch Extended Adjectival Projection. *Natural Language and Linguistic Theory* 15:289–368.

Corver, N. 1997b. *Much*-support as a last resort. *Linguistic Inquiry* 28:119–164.

Cowper, E. 1987. Pied Piping, Feature Percolation and the Structure of the Noun Phrase. *Canadian Journal of Linguistics* 34:321–338.

Demonte, V. 1995. Dative alternation in Spanish. *Probus* 7:5–30.

den Besten, H. 1977. On the interaction of root transformations and lexical deletive rules. Ms. University of Amsterdam. Expanded version published in W. Abraham ed. 1981. *On the Formal Syntax of the Westgermania: Papers from the 3rd Groningen Grammar Talks*, 47–131. Amsterdam; Philadelphia: John Benjamins.

den Dikken, M. 1995. *Particles: On the Syntax of Verb-Particle, Triadic, and Causative Constructions*. New York: Oxford University Press.

Doherty, C. 1993. Clauses Without *that*: The Case for Bare Sentential Complementation in English. Doctoral dissertation, University of California, Santa Cruz.

Doherty, C. 1996. Clausal Structure and the Modern Irish Copula. *Natural Language and Linguistic Theory* 14:1–46.

Doherty, C. 1997. Predicate Initial Constructions in Irish. *Proceedings of the Fifteenth West Coast Conference on Formal Linguistics*, 81–95. Stanford: CSLI Publications.

Downing, L. 1998. On the Prosodic Misalignment of Onset-less Syllables. *Natural Language and Linguistic Theory* 16:1–52.

Dowty, D. 1991. Thematic proto-roles and argument selection. *Language* 67:547–619.

Dubinsky, S. and K. Williams. 1995. Recategorization of Prepositions as Complementizers: The Case of Temporal Prepositions in English. *Linguistic Inquiry* 26:125–137.

Emonds, J. 1985. *A Unified Theory of Syntactic Categories*, Dordrecht: Foris.

Fassi Fehri, A. 1987. Generalized IP Structure, Case, Inflection, and VS Word Order. Ms., Faculty of Letters, Rabat.

Finer, D. 1997. Contrasting A'-dependencies in Selayarese. *Natural Language and Linguistic Theory* 15:677–728.

Fisher, C., H. Gleitman, and L. Gleitman. 1991. On the Semantic Content of Subcategorization Frames. *Cognitive Psychology* 23:331–392.

Fisher, C., D. Hall, S. Rackowitz and L. Gleitman. 1994. When it is Better to Receive than to Give: Structural and Semantic Supports for Verb Vocabulary Acquisition. *Lingua* 92:333–375. Reprinted in L. Gleitman and B. Landau eds. *The Acquisition of the Lexicon*, 333–375. MIT Press.

Fodor, J. 1970. Three Reasons for Not Deriving "kill" from "cause-to-die." *Linguistic Inquiry* 1:429–438.

Fodor, J., M. Garrett, E. Walker, and C. Parkes. 1980. Against Definitions. *Cognition* 8:263–267.

Franks, S. 1994. Parametric Properties of Numeral Phrases in Slavic. *Natural Language and Linguistic Theory* 12:599–674.

Fu, J., T. Roeper and H. Borer. 2001. The VP within process nominals: Evidence from adverbs and the VP anaphor *do so*. *Natural Language and Linguistic Theory* 19:549–582.

Fukui, N. 1986. A Theory of Category Projection and Its Applications. Doctoral dissertation, MIT.

Fukui, N. and M. Speas. 1986. Specifiers and Projection. In N. Fukui, T. Rappaport, and E. Sagey eds. *MIT Working Papers in Linguistics 8*, 128–172. Department of Linguistics, MIT.

Georgopoulos, C. 1987. Psych Nouns. *Proceedings of NELS 17*, 211–231. GLSA. University of Massachusetts at Amherst.

Ghomeshi, J. 1997. Non-projecting Nouns in Persian. *Natural Language and Linguistic Theory* 15:729–788.

Giorgi, A. and G. Longobardi. 1991. *The Syntax of Noun Phrases*. Cambridge; New York: Cambridge University Press.

Giusti, G. 1997. The Categorial Status of Determiners. In L. Haegeman ed. *The New Comparative Syntax*, 95–123. London, New York: Longman.

Gleitman, L. 1990. The Structural Sources of Verb Meanings. *Language Acquisition* 1:3–55.

Gleitman, L., H. Gleitman, C. Miller and R. Os-Trin. 1996. Similar, and Similar Concepts. *Cognition* 58:321–376.

Goldsmith, J. 1980. Meaning and Mechanism in Grammar. In S. Kuno ed. *Harvard Studies in Syntax and Semantics 3*, 423–448. Harvard University Department of Linguistics.

Green, G. 1974. *Semantics and Syntactic Regularity*. Bloomington: Indiana University Press.

Grimshaw, J. 1977. English Wh Constructions and the Theory of Grammar. Doctoral dissertation, University of Massachusetts at Amherst.

Grimshaw, J. 1979. Complement Selection and the Lexicon. *Linguistic Inquiry* 10:279–326.

Grimshaw, J. 1981. Form, Function, and the Language Acquisition Device. In C. L. Baker and J. McCarthy eds. *The Logical Problem of Language Acquisition*, 165–182. MIT Press.

Grimshaw, J. 1989. Getting the Dative Alternation. In I. Laka and A. Mahajan eds. *Functional Heads and Clause Structure, MIT Working Papers in Linguistics Volume 10*, 113–122. Department of Linguistics, MIT.

Grimshaw, J. 1990. *Argument Structure*. MIT Press.

Grimshaw, J. 1991. Extended Projection. Ms., Brandeis University.

Grimshaw, J. 1993. Semantic Structure and Semantic Content. Ms., Rutgers University.

Grimshaw, J. 1994. Lexical Reconciliation. *Lingua* 92:411–430. Reprinted in L. Gleitman and B. Landau eds. 1994. *The Acquisition of the Lexicon*, 411–430. MIT Press.

Grimshaw, J. 1997. Projection, Heads and Optimality. *Linguistic Inquiry* 28:373–422.

Grimshaw, J. 2000. Extended Projection and Locality. In P. Coopmans, M. Everaert and J. Grimshaw eds. *Lexical Specification and Insertion*, 115–133. Amsterdam; Philadelphia: John Benjamins.

Grimshaw, J. 2001. Economy of Structure in OT. ROA 434-0601, Rutgers Optimality Archive.

Grimshaw, J. 2003. Economy of Structure in OT. In A. Carpenter, A. Coetzee, and P. de Lacy eds. *Papers in Optimality Theory II*. University of Massachusetts Occasional Papers 26; GLSA, University of Massachusetts.

Grimshaw, J. In prep. Measure Nouns and Extended Projections.

Grimshaw, J. and S. Pinker. 1989. Positive and Negative Evidence in Language Acquisition. *Behavioral and Brain Sciences* 12:341–342.

Gropen, J., S. Pinker, M. Hollander, R. Goldberg and R. Wilson. 1989. The Learnability and Acquisition of the Dative Alternation in English. *Language* 65:203–257.

Grosu, A. 1996. The Proper Analysis of 'Missing-P' Free Relative Constructions. *Linguistic Inquiry* 27:257–293.

Guéron, J. and T. Hoekstra. 1988. T-chains and the constituent structure of auxiliaries. In A. Cardinaletti, G. Cinque and G. Giusti eds. *Constituent Structure: Papers from the 1987 Glow Conference*, 35–99. Dordrecht: Foris.

Haeberli, E. 1998. Categorial Feature Matrices and Checking. In *Proceedings of the North East Linguistic Society* 28:77–93. University of Massachusetts, GLSA.

Haeberli, E. 2001. Deriving Syntactic Effects of Morphological Case by Eliminating Abstract Case. *Lingua* 111:279–313.

Haeberli, E. 2002. *Features, Categories and the Syntax of A-Positions*. Dordrecht: Kluwer.

Haegeman, L. 1991. *Introduction to Government and Binding Theory*. Oxford; Cambridge, Mass.: Basil Blackwell.

Haegeman, L. 1995. *The Syntax of Negation*. New York: Cambridge University Press.

Haider, H. 1988. Matching Projections. In A. Cardinaletti, G. Cinque and G. Giusti eds. *Constituent Structure: Papers from the 1987 Glow Conference*, 101–121. Dordrecht: Foris.

Hellan, L. 1985. The Headedness of NPs in Norwegian. In P. Muysken and H. van Riemsdijk eds. *Features and Projections*, 89–122. Dordrecht: Foris.

Hendrick, R. 2000. Celtic Initials. In A. Carnie and E. Guilfoyle eds. *The Syntax of Verb Initial Languages*, 13–37. Oxford; New York: Oxford University Press.

Herslund, M. 1986. The Double Object Construction in Danish. In L. Hellan and K. Koch Christensen eds. *Topics in Scandinavian Syntax*, 125–147. Dordrecht: Kluwer.

Hestvik, A. 1991. Subjectless Binding Domains. *Natural Language and Linguistic Theory* 9:455–496.

Holmberg, A. 1986. Word order and Syntactic Features in the Scandinavian languages and English. Doctoral dissertation, University of Stockholm.

Holmberg, A. and C. Platzack. 1995. *The Role of Inflection in Scandinavian Syntax*. New York: Oxford University Press.

Horn, L. 1989. *A Natural History of Negation*. Chicago: University of Chicago Press.

Hornstein, N. 1977. S and X′ Convention. *Linguistic Analysis* 3:137–176.

Itô, J. and A. Mester. 1995. Japanese Phonology. In J. Goldsmith ed. *The Handbook of Phonological Theory*, 817–838. Cambridge, Mass.: Blackwell.

Itô, J. and A. Mester. 1999. The Structure of the Phonological Lexicon. In N. Tsujimura ed. *The Handbook of Japanese Linguistics*, 62–100. Malden Mass.; Oxford: Blackwell.

Jackendoff, R. 1972. *Semantic Interpretation in Generative Grammar*. MIT Press.

Jackendoff, R. 1973. The Base Rules for Prepositional Phrases. In S. Anderson and P. Kiparsky eds. *A Festschrift for Morris Halle*, 345–356. New York: Holt, Rinehart and Winston.

Jackendoff, R. 1977. *X-Bar Syntax: A Study of Phrase Structure*. MIT Press.

Jackendoff, R. 1990. *Semantic Structures*. MIT Press.

Jaeggli, O. 1986. Passive. *Linguistic Inquiry* 17:587–622.

Josefsson, G. 1993. Scandinavian pronouns and object shift. *Working Papers in Scandinavian Syntax* 52:1–28. Department of Scandinavian Linguistics, Lund.

Kager, R. 1995. The Metrical Theory of Word Stress. In J. Goldsmith ed. *The Handbook of Phonological Theory*, 367–402. Cambridge, Mass.: Blackwell.

Kathol, A. 2000. Syntactic Categories and Positional Shape Alternations. *Journal of Comparative Germanic Linguistics* 3:59–96.

Katz, N., E. Baker, and J. MacNamara. 1974. What's in a Name? A Study of How Children Learn Common and Proper Names. *Child Development* 45:469–473.

Kayne, R. 1981. On Certain Differences between French and English. *Linguistic Inquiry* 12:349–371.

Kayne, R. 1984. *Connectedness and Binary Branching*. Dordrecht; Cinnaminson: Foris.

Kayne, R. 1997. The English Complementizer *of*. *Journal of Comparative Germanic Linguistics* 1:43–54.

Kayne, R. 1998. A Note on Prepositions and Complementizers. In *Celebration: An Electronic Festschrift in honor of Noam Chomsky's 70th birthday*. MIT Press.

Kayne, R. 1999. Prepositional Complementizers as Attractors. *Probus* 11:39–73.

Kim, Y. 1994. A Non-Spurious Account of "Spurious" Korean Plurals. In Y.-K. Kim-Renaud ed. *Theoretical Issues in Korean Linguistics*, 303–324. Stanford: CSLI Publications.

Koopman, H. 1984. *The Syntax of Verbs*. Dordrecht: Foris.

Koster, J. 1978. Why Subject Sentences Don't Exist. In S. J. Keyser ed. *Recent Transformational studies of European Languages*, 53–64. MIT Press.

Koster, J. 1985. Reflexives in Dutch. In J. Guéron, H.-G. Obenauer and J.-Y. Pollock eds. *Grammatical Representation*, 141–167. Dordrecht: Foris.

Koster, J. 1987. *Domains and Dynasties*. Dordrecht: Foris.

Kratzer, A. 1996. Severing the External Argument from its Verb. In J. Rooryck and L. Zaring eds. *Phrase Structure and the Lexicon*, 109–137. Dordrecht; Boston: Kluwer.

Krifka, Manfred. 1999. Manner in Dative Alternation. In S. Bird, A. Carnie, J. Haugen and P. Norquest eds. *Proceedings of the 18th West Coast Conference on Formal Linguistics*, 260–271. Somerville, Mass.: Cascadilla Press.

Laka, M. I. 1990. Negation in Syntax: On the Nature of Functional Categories and Projections. Doctoral dissertation, MIT.

Landau, I. 2002. (Un)interpretable Neg in Comp. *Linguistic Inquiry* 33:465–492.

Larson, R. 1988. On the Double Object Construction. *Linguistic Inquiry* 19:335–391.

Larson, R. 1990. Extraction and Multiple Selection in PP. *The Linguistic Review* 7:169–182.

Lefebvre, C. and D. Massam 1988. Haitian Creole Syntax: A Case for *Det* as Head. *Journal of Pidgin and Creole Languages* 3:213–243.

Lefebvre, C. and P. Muysken. 1988. *Mixed Categories: Nominalizations in Quechua*. Dordrecht: Kluwer.

Levin, B. 1985. Lexical Semantics in Review: An Introduction. In B. Levin ed. *Lexical Semantics in Review*, 1–62. Lexicon Project Working Papers 1, Center for Cognitive Science, MIT.

Levin, B. and M. Rappaport Hovav. 1991. Wiping the Slate Clean: A Lexical Semantic Exploration. In B. Levin and S. Pinker eds. *Special Issue on Lexical and Conceptual Semantics, Cognition* 41:123–151.

Levin, B. and M. Rappaport Hovav. 1995. *Unaccusativity: At the Syntax-Lexical Semantics Interface.* MIT Press.

Li, Y. 1990. X^0-Binding and Verb Incorporation. *Linguistic Inquiry* 21:399–426.

Lobeck, A. 1990. Functional Heads as Proper Governors. *Proceedings of the Northeastern Linguistics Society 20*, 348–362. GLSA, University of Massachusetts at Amherst.

Longobardi, G. 1994. Reference and Proper Names: A Theory of N-movement in Syntax and Logical Form. *Linguistic Inquiry* 25:609–665.

MacNamara, J. 1982. *Names for Things: A Study of Human Learning.* MIT Press.

Maratsos, M. and M. A. Chalkley. 1981. The Internal Language of Children's Syntax: The Ontogenesis and Representation of Syntactic Categories. In K. Nelson ed., *Children's Language* 2:127–214. New York: Gardner Press.

Mazurkewich, I. and L. White. 1984. The Acquisition of the Dative Alternation: Unlearning Overgeneralization. *Cognition* 16:261–283.

McCarthy, J. 1982. Prosodic Structure and Expletive Infixation. *Language* 58:574–590.

McCarthy, J. and A. Prince. 1990. Foot and Word in Prosodic Morphology: the Arabic Broken Plural. *Natural Language and Linguistic Theory* 8:209–283.

McCarthy, J. and A. Prince. 1995. Prosodic Morphology. In J. Goldsmith ed. *The Handbook of Phonological Theory*, 318–366. Cambridge, Mass.: Blackwell.

McCarthy, J. and A. Prince. 1999. Faithfulness and Identity in Prosodic Morphology. In R. Kager, H. van der Hulst and W. Zonneveld eds. *The Prosody–Morphology Interface*, 218–309. Cambridge University Press.

McCloskey, J. and K. Hale. 1984 On the Syntax of Person–Number Inflection in Modern Irish. *Natural Language and Linguistic Theory* 1:487–533.

Morgan, J. and L. Travis. 1989. Limits on Negative Information in Language Input. *Journal of Child Language* 16:531–552.

Muysken, P. 1983. Parametrizing the Notion Head. *The Journal of Linguistic Research* 2:57–76.

Nakajima, H. 1991. Binding path and dependent categories. In Nakajima ed. *Current English Linguistics in Japan*, 289–344. Berlin; New York: Mouton de Gruyter.

Neeleman, A. and F. Weerman. 1999. *Flexible Syntax: A Theory of Case and Arguments.* Dordrecht: Kluwer.

Nespor, M. and I. Vogel. 1982. Prosodic Domains of External Sandhi Rules. In H. van der Hulst and N. Smith eds. *The Structure of Phonological Representations*, vol. 1, 222–255. Dordrecht: Foris.

Nespor, M. and I. Vogel. 1986. *Prosodic Phonology*. Dordrecht: Foris.

Oehrle, R. T. 1976. The Grammatical Status of the English Dative Alternation. Doctoral dissertation, MIT.

Ouhalla, J. 1990. Sentential Negation, Relativised Minimality and the Aspectual Status of Auxiliaries. *The Linguistic Review* 7:183–231.

Ouhalla, J. 1997. The Structure and Logical Form of Negative Sentences. *Linguistic Analysis* 27:220–244.

Pesetsky, D. 1982. Paths and Categories. Doctoral dissertation, MIT.

Pesetsky, D. 1995. *Zero Syntax: Experiencers and Cascades*. MIT Press.

Pesetsky, D. and E. Torrego. 2001. T-to-C Movement: Causes and Consequences. In M. Kenstowicz ed. *Ken Hale: A Life in Language*, 355–426. MIT Press.

Peters, P. S. 1972. The Projection Problem: How is a Grammar to be selected? In P. S. Peters ed. *Goals of Linguistic Theory*, 171–188. Englewood Cliffs, N.J.: Prentice-Hall

Pinker, S. 1979. Formal Models of Language Learning. *Cognition* 7:217–283.

Pinker, S. 1981. A Theory of the Acquisition of Lexical-Interpretive Grammars. In J. Bresnan ed. *The Mental Representation of Grammatical Relations*, 655–726. MIT Press.

Pinker, S. 1984. *Language Learnability and Language Development*. Harvard University Press.

Pinker, S. 1989. *Learnability and Cognition: The Acquisition of Argument Structure*. MIT Press.

Pinker, S. 1994. How Could a Child Use Verb Syntax to Learn Verb Semantics? *Lingua* 92:377–410. Reprinted in L. Gleitman and B. Landau eds. 1994. The Acquisition of the Lexicon, 377–410. MIT Press.

Pinker, S. and A. Prince. 1988. On Language and Connectionism: Analysis of a Parallel Distributed Processing model of language acquisition. *Cognition* 28:73–193. Reprinted in S. Pinker and J. Mehler (eds) *Connections and Symbols*. MIT Press.

Plann, S. 1986. "Substantive": A Neutralized Syntactic Category in Spanish. In I. Bordelois, H. Contreras and K. Zagona eds. *Generative Studies in Spanish Syntax*, 121–142. Dordrecht: Foris.

Pollock, J.-Y. 1989. Verb Movement, Universal Grammar and the Structure of IP. *Linguistic Inquiry* 20:365–424.

Postal, P. 1974. *On Raising: One Rule of English Grammar and its Theoretical implications*. MIT Press.

Potsdam. E. 1997. NegP and Subjunctive Complements in English. *Linguistic Inquiry* 28:533–541.

Radford, A. 1993. Head-hunting: On the Trail of the Nominal Janus. In G. Corbett, N. Fraser and S. McGlashan eds. *Heads in Grammatical Theory*, 73–113. Cambridge; New York: Cambridge University Press.

Rafel, J. 2001. As for *as/for*, they are semi-lexical heads. In Norbert Corver and Henk van Riemsdijk eds. *Semi-lexical categories*, 475–503. Mouton de Gruyter.

Randall, J. 1987. Indirect Positive Evidence: Overturning Overgeneralizations in Language Acquisition. Indiana Linguistics Club Publications.

Randall, J. 1990. Catapults and Pendulums: the Mechanics of Language Acquisition. *Linguistics* 28:381–406.

Reuland, E. 1986. A Feature System for the Set of Categorial Heads. In P. Muysken and H. van Riemsdijk eds. *Features and Projections*, 41–88. Dordrecht: Foris.

Ritter, E. 1987. NSO Noun Phrases in Modern Hebrew. *Proceedings of NELS 17*, 521–537. GLSA. University of Massachusetts at Amherst.

Ritter, E. 1991. Two Functional Categories in Noun Phrases, Evidence from Modern Hebrew. In S. Rothstein ed. *Perspectives on Phrase Structure: Heads and Licensing*, 37–62. San Diego: Academic Press.

Rivero, M.-L. 2000. Finiteness and Second Position in Long Verb Movement Languages: Breton and Slavic. In R. Borsley ed. *The Nature and Function of Syntactic Categories*, 295–323. San Diego: Academic Press.

Rizzi, L. 1990. Speculations on Verb Second. In J. Mascaro and M. Nespor eds. *Grammar in Progress, GLOW Essays for Henk van Riemsdijk*, 375–386. Dordrecht; Providence: Foris.

Rizzi, L. 1997. The Fine Structure of the Left Periphery. In L. Haegeman ed. *Elements of Grammar*, 281–337. Dordrecht; Boston: Kluwer.

Roberts, I. 1997. Restructuring, Head Movement and Locality. *Linguistic Inquiry* 28:423–460.

Rochette, A. 1988. Semantic and Syntactic Aspects of Romance Sentential Complementation. Doctoral dissertation, MIT.

Rochette, A. 1990. The Selectional Properties of Adverbs. In *Papers from the Twenty-Sixth Regional Meeting of the Chicago Linguistic Society vol. 1*, 379–391. Chicago Linguistic Society, University of Chicago.

Rosen, C. 1984. The Interface between Semantic Roles and Initial Grammatical Relations. In D. Perlmutter and C. Rosen eds. *Studies in Relational Grammar*, 38–77. Chicago: University of Chicago.

Rosen, S. T. 1989. Two Types of Noun Incorporation: A Lexical Analysis. *Language* 65:294–317.

Rosenbaum, P. 1967. *The Grammar of English Predicate Complement Constructions*. MIT Press.

Ross, J. R. 1967. Constraints on Variables in Syntax. Doctoral dissertation, MIT.

Rothstein, S. 1991. Heads, Projections, and Category Determination. In K. Leffel and D. Bouchard eds. *Views on Phrase Structure*, 97–112. Dordrecht; Boston: Kluwer.

Schwarzschild, R. 2002. The Grammar of Measurement. To appear in B. Jackson ed. *Proceedings of Semantics and Linguistic Theory XII*. Ithaca: CLC Publications, Department of Linguistics, Cornell University.

Selkirk, E. 1980a. Prosodic Domains in Phonology: Sanskrit Revisited. In M. Aronoff and M.-L. Kean eds. *Juncture*, 107–129. Saratoga, CA: Anma Libri.

Selkirk, E. 1980b. The Role of Prosodic Categories in English Word Stress. *Linguistic Inquiry* 11:563–605.

Smith, C. 1972. On Causative Verbs and Derived Nominals in English. *Linguistic Inquiry* 3:136–138.

Song, S. C. 1988. A Ubiquitous Plural Marker. In *Explorations in Korean Syntax and Semantics*, 19–23. Berkeley: Institute of East Asian Studies, University of California.

Stowell, T. 1981. Origins of Phrase Structure. Doctoral dissertation, MIT.

Suñer, M. 1991. Indirect Questions and the Structure of CP: Some Consequences. In H. Campos and F. Martínez-Gil eds. *Current Studies in Spanish Linguistics*, 283–312. Washington, D.C.: Georgetown University Press.

Talmy, L. 1985. Lexicalization Patterns: Semantic Structure in Lexical Forms. In T. Shopen ed. *Language Typology and Syntactic Description 3: Grammatical Categories and the Lexicon*, 57–149. Cambridge University Press.

Tenny, C. 1992. The Aspectual Interface Hypothesis. In I. Sag and A. Szabolcsi eds. *Lexical Matters*, 1–27. Stanford: CSLI Publications.

Tomioka, S. 1994. The Licensing of Lexical Projections. In E. Benedicto and J. Runner eds. *Functional Projections*, 209–226. University of Massachusetts Occasional Papers 17. Amherst, Massachusetts.

van Riemsdijk, H. 1978. *A Case Study in Syntactic Markedness: the Binding Nature of Prepositional Phrases*. Dordrecht: Foris.

van Riemsdijk, H. 1985. On Pied-piped Infinitives in German Relative Clauses. In Jindrich Toman ed. *Studies in German Grammar*, 165–192. Dordrecht: Foris.

van Riemsdijk, H. 1990. Functional Prepositions. In H. Pinkster and I. Geneé eds. *Unity in Diversity: Papers presented to Simon C. Dik on his 50th birthday*, 229–241. Dordrecht: Foris.

van Riemsdijk, H. 1998. Categorial Feature Magnetism: The Endocentricity and Distribution of Projections, *Journal of Comparative Germanic Linguistics* 2:1–48.

Van Valin, R. 1990. Semantic Parameters of Split Intransitivity. *Language* 66:221–260.

Vikner, S. 1995. *Verb Movement and Expletive Subjects in the Germanic Languages*. New York; Oxford: Oxford University Press.

Vos, R. 1999. A Grammar of Partitive Constructions. Tilburg Dissertation in Language Studies, Tilburg University.

Wasow, T. 1981. Comments on the Paper by Baker. In C. L. Baker and J. McCarthy eds. *The Logical Problem of Language Acquisition*, 324–329. MIT Press.

Williams, E. 1980. Abstract Triggers. *Journal of Linguistic Research* 1:71–82.

Williams, E. 1981a. Language Acquisition, Markedness and Phrase Structure. In S. Tavakolian ed. *Language Acquisition and Linguistic Theory*, 8–34. MIT Press.

Williams, E. 1981b. On the Notions "Head of a Word" and "Lexically Related." *Linguistic Inquiry* 12:245–274.

Zamparelli, R. 2000. *Layers in the Determiner Phrase*. New York: Garland.

Zanuttini, R. 1990. Two Types of Negative Markers. In J. Carter, R.-M. Dechaine, W. Philip, and T. Sherer eds. *Proceedings of NELS 20* 2:517–530. GLSA, University of Massachusetts.

Zanuttini, R. 1996. On the Relevance of Tense for Sentential Negation. In A. Belletti and L. Rizzi eds. *Parameters and Functional Heads: Essays in Comparative Syntax*, 181–207. New York: Oxford University Press.

Zanuttini, R. 1997. *Negation and clausal structure: A Comparative Study of Romance Languages*. New York: Oxford University Press.

Zaring, L. and P. Hirschbühler. 1997. Qu'est-ce que *ce que*? The diachronic evolution of a French complementizer. In A. van Kemenade and N. Vincent eds. *Parameters of Morphosyntactic Change*, 351–379. Cambridge University Press.

Zeller, J. 2001. Lexical Particles, Semi-lexical Postpositions. In N. Corver and H. van Riemsdijk eds. *Semi-lexical Categories*, 505–549. Berlin; New York: Mouton de Gruyter.

Zubizarreta, M.-L. 1987. *Levels of Representation in the Lexicon and Syntax*. Dordrecht: Foris.

Zwarts, J. 1992. X'-*Syntax and* X'-*Semantics*. Doctoral dissertation, Utrecht University. OTS dissertation series.

Zwarts, J. 1995. Lexical and Functional Direction in Dutch. In M. den Dikken and K. Hengeveld eds. *Linguistics in the Netherlands 1995*, 227–238. Amsterdam; Philadelphia: John Benjamins.

Zwicky, A. and G. Pullum. 1986. Two Spurious Counter Examples to the Principle of Phonology-free Syntax. *Ohio State University Working Papers in Linguistics* 32:92–99.

Index